THE
BEGINNING OF
ALL WISDOM

THE BEGINNING OF ALL WISDOM

TIMELESS ADVICE FROM THE ANCIENT GREEKS

STEVEN STAVROPOULOS

MARLOWE & COMPANY
NEW YORK

Published by
Marlowe & Company
An Imprint of Avalon Publishing Group, Incorporated
245 West 17th Street, 11th Floor
New York, NY 10011

Library of Congress Cataloging-in-Publication Data
The beginning of all wisdom : timeless advice from the ancient Greeks /
[compiled by] Steven Stavropoulos
p. cm.
Includes bibliographical references and index.
ISBN 1-56924-485-5
1. Quotations, Greek—Translations into English. I. Stavropoulos, Steven.

PN6080.B29 2003
089'.81—dc21
2003041276

9 8 7 6 5 4 3 2

Designed by Shona McCarthy
Map on p. viii by Mapping Specialists, Ltd.

Printed in the United States of America
Distributed by Publishers Group West

CONTENTS

GOD AND RELIGION

HUMANITY

EDUCATION AND LEARNING

ARTS AND SCIENCES

THE STATE

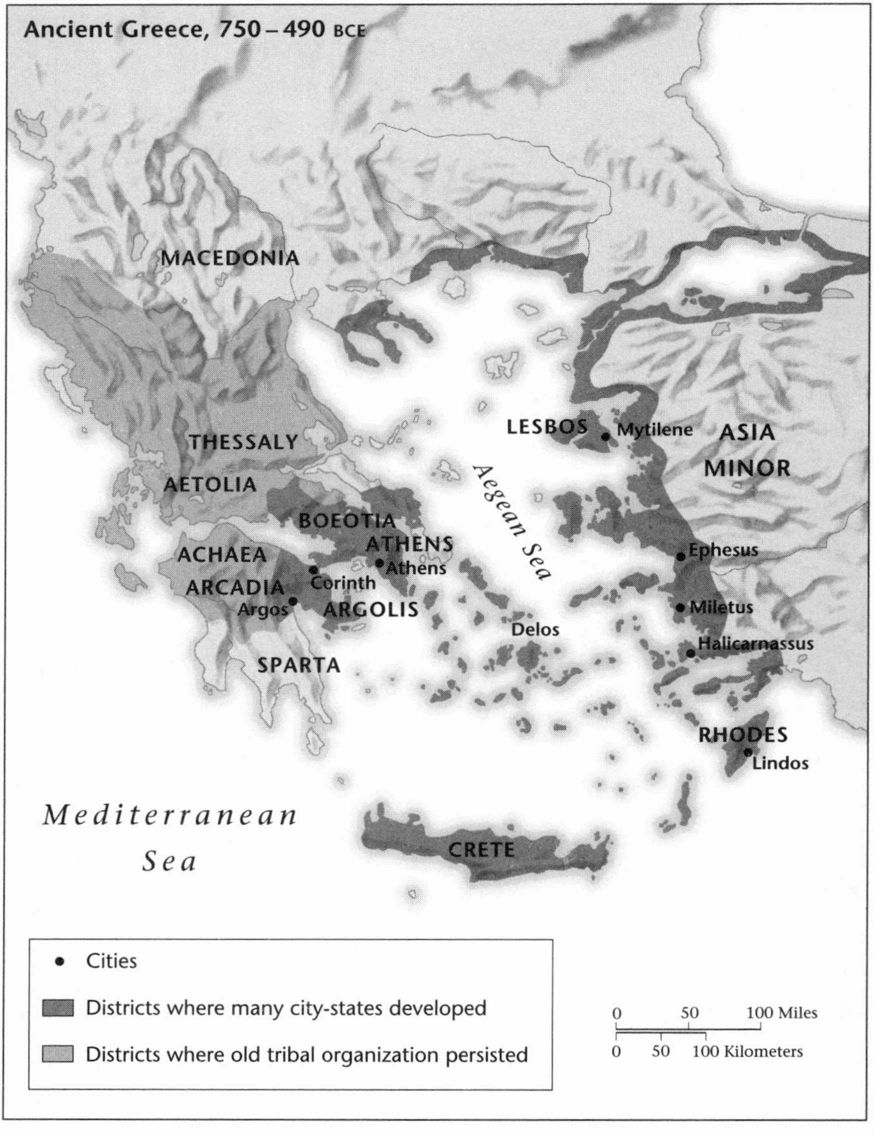
Ancient Greece, 750 – 490 BCE
MACEDONIA
THESSALY
AETOLIA
BOEOTIA
ATHENS
Athens
ACHAEA
ARCADIA
Corinth
Argos
ARGOLIS
SPARTA
LESBOS
Mytilene
ASIA
MINOR
Aegean Sea
Ephesus
Miletus
Delos
Halicarnassus
RHODES
Lindos
CRETE
Mediterranean
Sea
Cities
Districts where many city-states developed
Districts where old tribal organization persisted
0 50 100 Miles
0 50 100 Kilometers

INTRODUCTION

When the world is storm-driven and the bad that happens and the worse that threatens are so urgent as to shut out everything else from view, then we need to know all the strong fortresses of the spirit which men have built through the ages.

—Edith Hamilton, *The Greek Way*

It seems right that a book of quotations should start with one. Especially one that reminds us that in times of uncertainty we are not alone. Ours is an age of political upheaval, a time when excess threatens moderation and forces of prejudice and intolerance endanger the accomplishments of our fragile civilization.

As Edith Hamilton wrote in her masterwork, *The Greek Way,* tumultuous times like ours require spiritual fortresses. We need heroes. We learned on September 11, 2001, that the age of heroes is not dead. Heroes live among us like demigods in an old Greek myth. They are everyday people, like you and me, who value human dignity to such a degree, that they will rise to protect it, sometimes sacrificing themselves in the process. And they do it because they believe in themselves and the righteousness of their cause.

At the dawn of the twenty-first century, most citizens in the West might argue that this is our golden age. A time of accomplishments, magnificent discoveries, and innovation. Maybe they are right. But it is also a time of conflict and war. A time when we need to look deep inside ourselves and find the courage to stand up to challenges—in other words, to be heroic.

But in order to do this, we have to look back. Way back.

Greece, or Hellás as the Greeks have always called it, is a tiny country of fewer than 51,000 square miles located at the tip of the Balkan peninsula in southeastern Europe. It borders Turkey to the east; Albania, the Former Yugoslav Republic of Macedonia and Bulgaria to the north; and the Mediterranean Sea to the south. Greece's natural resources have always been scarce, and less of a quarter of its land is arable. The Greek landscape is ragged, full of hostile mountains, and surrounded by windswept archipelagoes. Yet, it was this deprived land that gave birth to democracy, philosophy, theater, poetry, sculpture, architecture, politics, and many other arts and sciences. What they didn't discover, the Greeks innovated. Strategically, thanks to its location, Greece has always been singular. Situated at the crossroads between Europe, Africa, and Asia, Greece has tempted world leaders who calculated that if they could subdue it, a door to other continents would open wide.

About 2,500 years ago, near the height of its civilization, Greece came under attack from the Persian Empire, a kingdom to the east of Greece stretching thousands of miles from Asia Minor—modern

Turkey—to India. Persia, with Darius I as its ruler, was a theocracy and the king—also known throughout the then-known world as the "Great King"—was believed to be a descendant of the gods. His rule over his subjects was absolute. His word final. His clothing royal and his abode unmatched in splendor and architecture. His army was immense—a swarming, crushing multitude of races, tongues, and weaponry.

The excess that defined their opponent was antithetical to everything the Greeks stood for. Poor, arid Greece was, nevertheless, the Greece of moderation, sufficiency, patriotism, and philosophy. It was a Greece of equals among equals, where a longing for independence ran as deep as the Aegean Sea and as high as heavenly Olympus. It was a Greece of scientific, literary, and military geniuses. They would share the world with Darius—but as neighbors, not as his slaves.

They resolved to stand up to the Persians and, if they had to, die fighting to defend their freedom. Throughout their struggle they never doubted they could defeat Darius and his minions; they believed in their virtuous cause. In a series of land and sea battles between 500 and 449 B.C.E., the tiny city-states of Greece dealt one devastating blow after another to Darius and his successors and gloriously defended their land from the attacking hordes. Today many historians and classicists agree that it was that triumph, and the Athenian Golden Age that followed it, that gave rise to civilization as we know it.

What was it that fortified the Greeks' spirits? Where did they find the strength to defeat an enemy hundreds of times stronger than themselves?

The answer can be found among the pages of *The Beginning of All Wisdom: Timeless Advice from the Ancient Greeks. The Beginning of All Wisdom* is a collection of sayings, proverbs, and maxims by ancient Greek philosophers, tragedians, scientists, politicians, generals, and poets. The reader will find practical advice on everyday problems but also answers to deep moral questions. And, through the sage reflections of those ancient Europeans, through a glimpse at the poems and philosophical axioms they were taught in school, we can espy their advanced civilization, measure ourselves against them, and find out whether we share their fortitude, their dreams, their bravery. We can find out who we are and how we can transcend ourselves; be more "Greek-like."

We will realize that as the Greeks were cosmopolitan and inclusive, so are we. We live and die in their democratic societies. We have stood up—many times when no one would—and defended freedom and equality. And, as is mentioned in our Constitution and shown in our history, we will sacrifice our lives for the preservation of our values.

In some ways this book is a testament not only to ancient Greece but to modern America as well. Because Greece's struggle has also been America's struggle: a constant campaign against the elements, against foreign threats, even against its very *self*. Just like

Greece, we have fought for freedom, equality, and survival. And we have survived. But we should not cease to remind ourselves how we got here or how we can do better. We should not forget Greece. A quotation comes to mind: "The numbing, benumbing thought that we owe nothing to Plato and Aristotle, nothing to the prophets who wrote the Bible, nothing to the generations who fought for freedoms activated in the Bill of Rights; we are basket cases of ingratitude, so many of us. We cannot hope to repay in kind what Socrates gave us, but to live [our] lives without any sense of obligation . . . is spiritually atrophying."*

In the end his book is about the power of the human spirit; this elemental force that changed the face of our planet. It's our human spirit that stands against intolerance and prejudice. It is our intellect and will, acting in concordance with virtue, that have given us strength, time and again, to counter evil.

The Beginning of All Wisdom contains almost 888 quotations, which I have compiled from 132 sources. The ancient Greek poets, writers, dramatists, and philosophers wrote extensively and profusely. The hunting and gathering of their most quotable lines required my doing hundreds of hours of research and making countless visits to libraries and bookstores. In order to reap the fruits

---

* William F. Buckley, Jr., speech at a testimonial dinner, on receipt of the Julius Award from the School of Public Administration, UCLA, March 21, 1990.

of Aristotle's fecund mind, I had to stroll, like a student in that old peripatetic Academy of Plato, through renowned and highly complex works such as *Nicomachean Ethics, Metaphysics, Eudemian Ethics, Poetics, Politics,* and many other treatises. I found that Aristotle explored and conversed on just about every topic within human experience. His writing is clear-cut, precise, and methodical. His wisdom immense. Aristotle's strongest aptitude was his will to discover the truth. I realized that in doing so he even went up against his great teacher, Plato.*

Plato and his mentor, Socrates, laid the foundations of philosophy as we know it today. "The safest general characterization of the European philosophical tradition is that it consists of a series of footnotes to Plato."† Assembling *The Beginning of All Wisdom* was an opportunity for me to be a jubilant participant in Plato's *Symposium* and a juror in his *Apology* of Socrates. I had to follow the great master in his quest to build the perfect Republic and hear him discuss justice and the citizen's obligations toward the constitution in *Laws.*

But it was also an opportunity to find myself in the open theaters of ancient Athens, where Euripides with his ageless *Medea* tried to surpass Aeschylus' masterpiece *Prometheus Bound* and Sophocles' amaranthine hymn to freedom, *Antigone.*

Furthermore, I had to be an Athenian policy-maker and hear

---

* See what Aristotle says about Plato and truth under the heading *Truth.*
† Alfred North Whitehead. Process and Reality. (New York: Macmillan, 1929).

Demosthenes, one of the greatest orators of all time, expound in his *Philippics,* his speeches against King Philip II of the Greek city-state of Macedonia, the reasons that Athens should remain independent and not unify with Macedonia under an umbrella of city-states known as Hellás. Fortunately for Hellás, it was Philip who succeeded in this argument and not Demosthenes. Upon Philip's death in 336 B.C.E., his son, Alexander the Great, having a unified Greece behind him, began his quest to spread Hellenic culture and language throughout Asia and the then-known world.

Anyone who has ever read world history will remember the Spartans, their strict—almost militaristic—way of life, and their tremendous courage. (Here I have to admit that when it comes to Sparta, I may be a little prejudiced, being a descendant of Spartans myself—my father, Nicholas, was born within the borders of the once-great city.) In order to understand those celebrated citizen-warriors, I had to read through Plutarch's *Lives* and *Sayings of Spartans.* I had to observe their customs and listen to their notions of liberty, honor, and courage in order to understand just how in 480 B.C.E. the Spartan king Leonidas with an army of just 300 soldiers decided to take on thousands of Persians at the Battle of Thermopylae.

There, by sacrificing their lives for Greece, the Spartans delayed the Persian army, thus giving a chance to their Greek compatriots to mobilize their forces. It was the day "King Leonidas and his three hundred" trod as immortals the threshold of human history. Today, when we decide to make a heroic stand—as we did in the Alamo—we bring the three hundred of Thermopylae as an example of courage and sacrifice.

But in order to better understand notions such as liberty and freedom, I had to read the philosophies of Heracleitus, Anaximander, Thales, Epictetus, and Epicurus. And, yes, I had to listen to that immortal bard, Homer, as he took me on a mythical voyage throughout the then-known cosmos with his hero Odysseus on his quest to reach his homeland, Ithaca. I had to converse with Diogenes the Cynic and listen to his arguments for unadorned and unfettered living.

The sources of ancient Greek thought are inexhaustible. For the reader who is interested in reading the original Greek text, Harvard University Press's Loeb Classical Library is a series of books that offer ancient Greek and Latin texts alongside an English translation. Of course, a knowledge of ancient or modern Greek always helps. In fact, I translated some of the quotations in this book from the original Greek. There are many other series, such as the Penguin Classics, in which readers can immerse themselves in ancient Greek wisdom. As statues in museums reveal to the visitor a long-forgotten beauty and clarity of art, the ideas and inspirations of the ancient Greeks speak with simplicity and lucidity to the reader. Their only demand, their only desire, is for someone to liberate them from the dust and rust of time.

It is my hope that readers of *The Beginning of All Wisdom: Timeless Advice from the Ancient Greeks* benefit from this book in more than one way. We can find answers to the predicaments daily living imposes on us. We can ponder the need to coexist peacefully, the need to respect one another's religions, ideals, and values. We can find moral direction. Finally, we can use these words of wisdom to catch a glimpse of the marvelous era that gave us life, fortified our ideals, and gave us strength to become masters of our times—and to set sail for the greatest of discoveries: that of ourselves.

THE
BEGINNING OF
ALL WISDOM

VIRTUE

AMBITION

Men's ambition and their desire to make money are among the most frequent causes of deliberate acts of injustice.
> —**Aristotle,** *Politics*

Slight not what is near through aiming at what is far.
> —**Euripides,** *Rhesus*

Shoals of corpses shall witness, mute,
even to generations to come,
before the eyes of men that we ought never,
being mortal, to cast our sights too high.
> —**Aeschylus,** *The Persians*

My father will leave nothing for me to do.

> —Alexander the Great, *Sayings of Kings and Commanders I* (As a child, commenting on his father's military successes in Asia)

ANGER

We should praise a person who feels angry on the right grounds and against the right persons and also in the right manner at the right moment and for the right length of time.

> —Aristotle, *Nicomachean Ethics*

Whoever grows angry amid troubles applies a drug worse than the disease and is a physician unskilled about misfortunes.

> —Sophocles

Wherefore the sick, the necessitous, [those at war,] the lovesick, the thirsty, in a word, all who desire something and cannot obtain it, are prone to anger and easily excited, especially against those who make light of their present condition; for instance, the sick man is easily provoked in regard to his illness, the necessitous in regard to his poverty, the warrior in regard to warlike affairs, the lover in regard to love affairs, and so with all the rest; for the passion present in his mind in each case paves the way for his anger.

—**Aristotle,** *Rhetoric*

ARROGANCE

Zeus detests above all the boasts of a proud tongue.

—**Sophocles,** *Antigone*

Arrogance is an impediment to wisdom.

—**Bias of Priene, fragment**

Whoever thinks that he alone has speech, or possesses speech or mind above others, when unfolded such men are seen to be empty.

—**Sophocles,** *Antigone*

Wit is educated insolence.

—**Aristotle,** *Rhetoric*

For insolence, once blossoming, bears its fruit,
a bushel of doom, from which it reaps a tear-filled harvest.

—**Aeschylus,** *The Persians*

Search well and be wise, nor believe that self-willed pride will ever be better than good counsel.

—Aeschylus, *Prometheus Bound*

CHARACTER DEVELOPMENT

Character is destiny.

—Heraclitus, fragment

As it is the nature of the body to be developed by appropriate exercises, it is the nature of the soul to be developed by moral precepts.

—Isocrates, letter to Demonicus

It is not the oath that makes us believe the man, but the man the oath.

—Aeschylus, fragment

Only perform such acts as you will not regret later.

—Pythagoras

In every one of us there are two ruling and directing principles, whose guidance we follow wherever they may lead; the one being an innate desire of pleasure; the other, an acquired judgment which aspires after excellence.

—Socrates, as quoted in Plato's *Phaedrus*

Badness can be got easily and in shoals; the road to her is smooth, and she lives very near us. But between us and Goodness the gods have placed the sweat of our brows; long and steep is the path that leads to her.

—Hesiod, *Works and Days*

Never hope to conceal any shameful thing which you have done; for even if you do conceal it from others, your own heart will know.

—Isocrates, letter to Demonicus

There is no more important lesson to be learned or habit to be formed than that of right judgment and of delighting in good characters and noble actions.

—Aristotle, *Politics*

Fear the gods, honor your parents, respect your friends, obey the laws.

—Isocrates, letter to Demonicus

We ought to do everything both cautiously and confidently at the same time.

—Epictetus, *Discourses*

Let not sleep e'er close thy tired eyes without thou ask thyself:
What have I omitted and what done? Abstain thou if 'tis evil;
persevere if good.

  —**Pythagoras**

You should not consider a man's age but his acts.

  —**Sophocles,** *Antigone*

COMPASSION

No act of kindness, no matter how small, is ever wasted.

  —**Aesop,** *Fables*

Kindness is ever the begetter of kindness.

  —**Sophocles,** *Ajax*

If we always helped one another, no one would need luck.

  —**Menander**

It is the task of a good man to help those in misfortune.

  —**Sophocles, fragment**

He who cares for his brother, cares for himself.

　　—Xenophon

Words are the physicians of a mind diseased.

　　—Aeschylus, *Prometheus Bound*

In generosity we are equally singular, acquiring our friends by conferring, not by receiving, favors. Yet, of course, the doer of the favor
is the firmer friend of the two, in order by continued kindness to
keep the recipient in his debt; while the debtor feels less keenly
from the very consciousness that the return he makes will be a
payment, not a free gift.

　　—Pericles, "Funeral Oration," as quoted in Thucydides'
　　The History of the Peloponnesian War

CONDEMNATION AND PREJUDICE

In your sex-life preserve purity, as far as you can, before marriage,
and, if you indulge, take only those privileges which are lawful.
However, do not make yourself offensive, or censorious, to those
who do indulge, and do not make frequent mention of the fact
that you do not yourself indulge.

　　—Epictetus, *Enchiridion*

COURAGE

Heroes have the whole earth for their tomb.

—Pericles, "Funeral Oration," as quoted in Thucydides'
The History of the Peloponnesian War

To persevere, trusting in what hopes he has, is courage in a man.

—Euripides, *Heracles*

The bravest are surely those who have the clearest vision of what is before them, glory and danger alike, and, notwithstanding, go out to face it.

—Thucydides, *The History of the Peloponnesian War*

A man is not brave if he endures formidable things through ignorance (for instance, if owing to madness he were to endure a flight of thunderbolts), nor if he does so owing to passion when knowing the greatness of the danger, as the Celts "take arms and march against the waves"; and in general, the courage of barbarians has an element of passion.

—Aristotle, *Eudemian Ethics*

Courage makes men perform noble acts in the midst of dangers according to the dictates of the law and in submission to it; the contrary is cowardice.

—Aristotle, *Rhetoric*

Danger gleams like sunshine to a brave man's eyes.
> —Euripides, *Iphigenia in Tauris*

Brave hearts do not back down.
> —Sophocles

Physical strength is movement of the soul assisted by the body.
> —Socrates

Courage [is] to be undismayed by fears of death and be confident in alarms and brave in face of dangers, and to prefer a fine death to base security, and to be a cause of victory. It also belongs to courage to labor and endure and play a manly part. Courage is accompanied by confidence and bravery and daring, and also by perseverance and endurance.
> —Aristotle, *Virtues and Vices*

The brave endure their labors, the cowardly are worth nothing at all.
> —Euripides, *Iphigenia in Tauris*

Strive by all means to live in security, but if ever it falls to your lot to face the dangers of battle, seek to preserve your life, but with honor and not with disgrace; for death is the sentence which fate has passed on all mankind, but to die nobly is the special honor which nature has reserved for the good.
> —Isocrates, letter to Demonicus

Those who cannot bravely face danger are the slaves of their attackers.

—Aristotle, *Politics*

When a man does not shrink from a deed, he is not scared by a word.

—Sophocles, *Oedipus Tyrannus*

These are the Spartans' walls.

—King Agesilaus II of Sparta, pointing to Spartan soldiers, upon being asked why Sparta had no walls to protect it from invasions, as quoted in Plutarch's *Sayings of Spartans*

Fortune is not on the side of the fainthearted.

—Sophocles, *Phaedra*

Don't you realize that war has need, not of those who run away, but of those who stand their ground?

—King Agesilaus II of Sparta, upon hearing a lame Spartan soldier heading to battle ask a man to sell him a horse, as quoted in Plutarch's *Sayings of Spartans*

He is the best man who, when making his plans, fears and reflects on everything that can happen to him, but in the moment of action is bold.

—Herodotus, *Histories*

The Spartans do not ask how many are the enemy but where are they.

—King Agis of Sparta, as quoted in Plutarch's *Sayings of Spartans*

I think that just as one man's body is naturally stronger than another's for labour, so one man's soul is naturally braver than another's in danger. For I notice that men brought up under the same laws and customs differ widely in daring.

> —Socrates, as quoted in Xenophon's *Memorabilia*

The young men are the walls of Sparta, and the points of their spears its boundaries.

> —King Antalcidas of Sparta, as quoted in Plutarch's *Sayings of Spartans*

Come and take them . . .

> —King Leonidas of Sparta, upon being asked by King Xerxes of Persia to hand over his arms, as quoted in Plutarch's *Sayings of Spartans*

DECEPTION

Appearances are often deceiving.

> —Aesop, *Fables*

I have learned to hate all traitors,
and there is no disease that I spit on more than treachery.

> —Aeschylus, *Prometheus Bound*

Bear in mind that while the base may be pardoned for acting without principle, since it is on such a foundation that from the first their lives have been built, yet the good may not neglect virtue without subjecting themselves to rebukes from many quarters; for all men despise less those who do wrong than those who have claimed to be respectable and yet are in fact no better than the common run; and rightly, too, for when we condemn those who deceive us in words alone, how, pray, can we deny the baseness of those who in their whole lives belie their promise?

—Isocrates, letter to Demonicus

DETERMINATION AND WILL

Words are but the shadows of actions.

—Democritus, as quoted in Plutarch's *Of the Training of Children.*

It is difficulties that show what men are.

—Epictetus, *Discourses*

Consider at what price you sell your freedom of will. If you must sell it, man, at least do not sell it cheap.

—Epictetus, *Discourses*

Bear and forbear.

—Epictetus, fragments

Our aim is not to know what courage is but to be courageous, not to know what justice is but to be just, in the same way as we want to be healthy rather than to ascertain what health is, and to be in good condition of body rather than to ascertain what good bodily condition is.

—Aristotle, *Eudemian Ethics*

Fortune is unstable, while our will is free.

—Epicurus, fragment

Self-will in the man who does not reckon wisely is by itself the weakest of all things.

—Aeschylus, *Prometheus Bound*

The beginning is more than half the whole task.

—Aristotle, *Ethics*

We have a man who does not boast, but whose hand sees what must be done.

—Aeschylus, *Seven Against Thebes*

Reason is not measured by size or height, but by principle.

—Epictetus, *Discourses*

EQUALITY

By law a man is free and another slave. But by nature there is no difference between them. That's why such a relationship is not just but, rather, violent.

—**Aristotle,** *Politics*

All men believe that justice means equality.

—**Aristotle,** *Politics*

It is clear that not in one thing alone, but in many ways equality and freedom of speech are a good thing.

—**Herodotus,** *Histories*

Inequality is everywhere at the bottom of faction, for, in general, faction arises from men's striving for what is equal.

—**Aristotle,** *Politics*

Every creature is better or worse because of its own particular virtue or vice. Can it be, then, that man is the only creature without a special virtue, but he must have recourse to his hair, and his clothes, and his [family name]?

—**Epictetus, fragments**

If we look to [our] laws, they afford equal justice to all in their private differences; if no social standing, advancement in public life falls to reputation for capacity, class considerations not being allowed to interfere with merit; nor again does poverty bar the way. If a man is able to serve the state, he is not hindered by the obscurity of his condition.

—Pericles, "Funeral Oration," as quoted in Thucydides'
The History of the Peloponnesian War

The art of being a slave is to rule one's master.

—Diogenes of Sinope, fragment

Equality will never be found among humans.

—Euripides

FEAR

Cowards do not count in battle; they are there, but not in it.

—Euripides, fragment

Most of men are naturally apt to be swayed by fear rather than reverence, and to refrain from evil rather because of the punishment that it brings than because of its own foulness.

—Aristotle, *Nicomachean Ethics*

The coward calls the brave man rash; the rash man calls him a coward.

　—**Aristotle,** *Nicomachean Ethics*

Cowardice [is] to be easily excited by chance alarms, and especially by fear of death or of bodily injuries, and to think it better to save oneself by any means than to meet a fine end. Cowardice is accompanied by softness, unmanliness, faint-heartedness, fondness of life; and it also has an element of cautiousness and submissiveness of character.

　—**Aristotle,** *Virtues and Vices*

To him who is afraid, everything rustles.

　—**Sophocles,** *Acrisius*

Why should he who is scared be careful?

　—**Menander**

FLATTERY

Abhor flatterers as you would deceivers; for both, if trusted, injure those who trust them. If you admit as friends men who seek your favor for the lowest ends, your life will be lacking in friends who will risk your displeasure for the highest good.

　—**Isocrates, letter to Demonicus**

A tyrant is really nothing but a slave since he accepts flattery and deceit and in turn flatters those who are base. A trait of a tyrant is never to know true freedom nor true friendship.

—**Plato,** *The Republic*

Most men like flattery, for a flatterer is a friend who is your inferior, or pretends to be so, and to love you more than you love him; but to be loved is felt to be nearly the same as to be honored, which most people covet.

—**Aristotle,** *Nicomachean Ethics*

One may justly take you to task because, while you know well that many great houses have been ruined by flatterers and while in your private affairs you abhor those who practice this art, in your public affairs you are not so minded towards them; on the contrary, while you denounce those who welcome and enjoy the society of such men, you yourselves make it manifest that you place greater confidence in them than in the rest of your fellow citizens.

—**Isocrates,** *On the Peace* **(addressing the Athenian public)**

FREEDOM

He is free who lives as he wills, who is subject neither to compulsion, nor hindrance, nor force, whose choices are unhampered, whose desires attain their end, whose aversions do not fall into what they would avoid.

—Epictetus, *Discourses*

No one is free except Zeus.

—Aeschylus, *Prometheus Bound*

War is the father of all and king of all, and some he shows as gods, others as men; some he makes slaves, others free.

—**Heraclitus, as quoted by Hippolytus**

You know a free man because he tells the truth.

—**Menander, fragment**

It is a noble thing to fight that one may never be in danger of becoming a slave.

—**Xenophon,** *Cyropaedia*

Do you think that a man is happy when he's a slave and allowed to do nothing he desires?

—**Socrates, as quoted in Plato's** *Lysis*

No one is free, who is not master of himself.

—**Pythagoras**

GARRULITY

Misery is the end of those with unbridled mouths.
> —**Euripides,** *Bacchants*

A man who takes pleasure in speaking continuously fools himself in thinking he is not unpleasant to those around him.
> —**Sophocles**

Nature has given us one tongue and two ears so that we would listen twice as much as we speak.
> —**Zeno of Elea**

Always when you are about to say anything, first weigh it in your mind; for with many the tongue outruns the thought. Let there be but two occasions for speech—when the subject is one which you thoroughly know and when it is one on which you are compelled to speak. On these occasions alone is speech better than silence; on all others, it is better to be silent than to speak.
> —**Isocrates, letter to Demonicus**

Speak not nor act before thou hast reflected.
> —**Pythagoras**

Wise is he who can compress many thoughts into few words.
> —**Aristophanes,** *The Thesmophoriazusae*

Consider before acting, to avoid foolishness: It is the worthless man who speaks and acts thoughtlessly.

—**Pythagoras**

GLORY

It is men who endure toil and dare dangers that achieve glorious deeds, and it is a lovely thing to live with courage and to die leaving behind an everlasting renown.

—**Alexander the Great, as quoted in Plutarch's** *Lives*

The nearest way to glory is to strive to be what you wish to be thought to be.

—**Socrates**

Achilles absent was Achilles still.

—**Homer,** *The Iliad*

Glory in excess is fraught with peril; the lofty peak is struck by Zeus' thunderbolt.

—**Aeschylus,** *Agamemnon*

Toil, says the proverb, is the sire of fame.

—**Euripides, fragment**

I see that my funeral rites will be imposing.

> —**Alexander the Great, on his deathbed, as quoted in**
> Plutarch's *Sayings of Kings and Commanders*

Would you rather be the victor at the Olympic games or the announcer of the victor?

> —**Themistocles, upon asked whether he would have**
> **preferred to have been Achilles or Homer, as quoted**
> **in Plutarch's** *Sayings of Kings and Commanders*

If I have done any goodly deed, that shall be my memorial; but if not, then not all the statues in the world, the works of menial and worthless men, will avail.

> —**King Agesilaus of Sparta, on his deathbed, as quoted**
> **in Plutarch's** *Sayings of Spartans*

The admiration of the present and succeeding ages will be ours, since we have not left our power without witness, but have shown it by mighty proofs; and far from needing a Homer for our panegyrist, or other of his craft whose verses might charm for the moment only for the impression which they gave to melt at the touch of fact, we have forced every sea and land to be the highway of our daring, and everywhere, whether for evil or for good, have left imperishable monuments behind us. Such is the Athens for which these men, in the assertion of their resolve not to lose her, nobly fought and died; and well may every one of their survivors be ready to suffer in her cause.

> —**Pericles, "Funeral Oration," as quoted in Thucydides'**
> *The History of the Peloponnesian War*

GOOD AND EVIL

Externals are not under my control; moral choice is under my control. Where am I to look for the good and the evil? Within me, in that which is my own.

—**Epictetus,** *Discourses*

There [is] one only good, namely, knowledge; and one only evil, namely, ignorance.

—**Socrates, as quoted in Diogenes Laërtius'** *Lives of Eminent Philosophers*

The essence of good and evil is a certain disposition of the will.

—**Epictetus,** *Of Courage*

In the world of knowledge, the essential Form of Good is the limit of our inquiries, and can barely be perceived. However, when perceived, we cannot help concluding that it is in every case the source of all that is bright and beautiful—in the visible world giving birth to light and its master, and in the intellectual world dispensing, immediately and with full authority, truth and reason— and that whosoever would act wisely, either in private or in public, must set this Form of Good before his eyes.

—**Socrates, as quoted in Plato's** *The Republic*

No one who errs unwillingly is evil.

—**Sophocles, fragment**

Two urns by Jove's high throne have ever stood,—
The source of evil one, and one of good.
>   —**Homer,** *The Iliad*

GREED AND DISHONEST PROFITS

It is more necessary to equalize appetites than possessions, and that can only be done by adequate education under the laws.
>   —**Aristotle,** *Politics*

Nothing is sufficient for the person who finds sufficiency too little.
>   —**Epicurus, fragment**

Of meanness [of character] there are three kinds: love of base gain, parsimony, niggardliness. Love of base gain makes men seek profit from all sources and pay more regard to the profit than to the disgrace; parsimony makes them unwilling to spend money on a necessary object; niggardliness causes them only to spend in driblets and in a bad way, and to lose more than they gain by not at the proper moment letting go the difference. It belongs to meanness to set a very high value on money and to think nothing that brings profit a disgrace—a menial and servile and squalid mode of life, alien to ambition and to liberality. Meanness is accompanied by pettiness, sulkiness, self-abasement, lack of proportion, ignobleness, misanthropy.

—**Aristotle,** *Virtues and Vices*

Try to make of money a thing to use as well as to possess; it is a thing of use to those who understand how to enjoy it, and a mere possession to those who are able only to acquire it. Prize the substance you have for two reasons—that you may have the means to meet a heavy loss and that you may go to the aid of a worthy friend when he is in distress; but for your life in general, cherish your possessions not in excess but in moderation.

—**Isocrates, letter to Demonicus**

In the case of natural desires few people go wrong and only in one way, in the direction of too much.

—**Aristotle,** *Ethics*

Luxury and avarice have similar results.

—**Pythagoras**

The hope of dishonest profit is the beginning of loss.

—**Menander**

You should gain riches honestly. Ill-gained profits have brought destruction to many.

—**Euripides**

Do not gain basely; base gain is equal to ruin.

—Hesiod, *Works and Days*

Prefer honest poverty to unjust wealth; for justice is better than riches in that riches profit us only while we live, while justice provides us glory even after we are dead; and while riches are shared by bad men, justice is a thing in which the wicked can have no part.

—Isocrates, letter to Demonicus

When from an evil action you have gained profits, know that you have married misery.

—Menander

Riches that are the fruit of dishonest labor are full of shame.

—Democritus

Riches and honors easily acquired, are easy thus to lose.

—Pythagoras

Evil profits damage virtue.

—Democritus

Riches do not protect the man who in wantonness has kicked the mighty altar of Justice into obscurity.

—Aeschylus, *Agamemnon*

In a rich man's house there is no place to spit but his face.

—**Diogenes of Sinope, fragment**

HABIT

Character is simply habit long continued.

—**Plutarch,** *Morals*

It is a matter of no little importance what sort of habits we form from the earliest age—it makes a vast difference, or rather all the difference in the world.

—**Aristotle,** *Ethics*

To do the same thing over and over again is not only boredom: It is to be controlled by, rather than controling, what you do.

—**Heraclitus, fragment**

If you want to do something, make a habit of it; if you want not to do something, refrain from doing it, and accustom yourself to something else instead.

—**Epicetus,** *Discourses*

How does a person who cannot tame his desires differ from the most ignorant beast?

—**Xenophon,** *Memorabilia*

The moral virtues are produced in us neither by nature nor against nature. Nature prepares in us the ground for their reception, but their complete formation is the product of habit.

—**Aristotle,** *Ethics*

What reinforcements, then, is it possible to find with which to oppose habit? Why, the contrary habit.

—**Epictetus,** *Discourses*

We are more sensible of what is done against custom than against nature.

—**Plutarch, Morals**

HONOR

Consider your honor, as a gentleman, of more weight than an oath. Never tell a lie. Pay attention to matters of importance.

—**Solon, as quoted in Diogenes Laërtius'** *Lives of Eminent Philosophers*

Love of honor is a very shady sort of possession.

—Herodotus, *Histories*

If you had any knowledge of the noble things of life, you would refrain from coveting others' possessions; but for me to die for Greece is better than to be the sole ruler over the people of my race.

—**King Leonidas of Sparta, upon asked by King Xerxes of Persia to let the Persian army pass through Thermopylae in exchange for Leonidas' crowning as sole ruler of Greece after Greece's defeat, as quoted in Plutarch's** *Sayings of Spartans*

In meat and drink and sleep and sex all creatures alike seem to take pleasure; but love of honor is rooted neither in the brute beasts nor in every human being.

—**Xenophon,** *Hiero*

When a man gives way to pleasures contrary to the counsel and commendation of the lawgiver, he is by no means conferring honor on his soul, but rather dishonor, by loading it with woes and remorse.

—**Plato,** *Laws*

Athenians excel all others not so much in singing or in stature or in strength, as in love of honor, which is the strongest incentive to deeds of honor and renown.

—**Xenophon,** *Memorabilia*

There is hardly a man of us all who pays honor rightly, although he fancies he does so; for honor paid to a thing divine is beneficent, whereas nothing that is maleficent confers honor; and he that thinks to magnify his soul by words or gifts or obeisances, while he is improving it no whit in goodness, fancies indeed that he is paying it honor, but in fact does not do so.

—Plato, *Laws*

Honor, speaking generally, consists in following the better, and in doing our utmost to effect the betterment of the worse, when it admits of being bettered.

—Plato, *Laws*

JUSTICE AND INJUSTICE

The tyranny imposed on the soul by anger, or fear, or lust, or pain, or envy, or desire, I generally call "injustice."

—Plato, *Laws*

Don't appear just; be just.

—Aeschylus

It is the way that we behave in our dealings with other people that makes us just or unjust, and the way that we behave in the face of danger, accustoming ourselves to be timid or confident, that makes us brave or cowardly.

—**Aristotle,** *Ethics*

The duty of the virtuous men is to serve justice and to always, in every occasion, punish the evil ones.

—**Euripides,** *Hecuba*

If you expect to stop denunciation of your wrong way of life by putting people to death, there is something amiss with your reasoning. This way of escape is neither possible nor creditable; the best and easiest way is not to stop the mouths of others, but to make yourselves as well-behaved as possible.

—**Socrates, as quoted in Plato's** *Apology*

Injustice is an act that disregards all laws.

—**Plato**

The question what rules of conduct should govern the relations between husband and wife, and generally between friend and friend, seems to be ultimately a question of justice.

—**Aristotle,** *Nicmachean Ethics*

Among all willing injustices, most occur out of greed and ambition.

—**Aristotle,** *Politics*

The worst case of injustice is for someone to believe he is just while he is not.

> —Plato, *The Republic*

When you act justly you have the gods as allies.

> —Menander, fragment

In the state where court cases and great injustices abound, citizens will never become friends.

> —Plato, *Laws*

A system of morality which is based on relative emotional values is a mere illusion, a thoroughly vulgar conception which has nothing sound in it and nothing true.

> —Plato, *Phaedo*

If you have done terrible things, you must endure terrible things; for thus the sacred light of injustice shines bright.

> —Sophocles, *Ajax*

Where injustice doesn't exist, citizens are philanthropists.

> —Menander

Unjust living is not only more shameful and wicked than righteous living but also more unpleasant for those engaged in it.

> —Plato, *Laws*

The city where everyone curses and does as he pleases will eventually disappear from the face of the earth.

—Sophocles, *Ajax*

The only time an unjust man will scream against injustice is when he is afraid someone will practice it on him.

—Plato, *The Republic*

The unjust will never be able to create something in unison.

—Plato, *The Republic*

Justice turns the scale, bringing to some learning through suffering.

—Aeschylus, *Agamemnon*

People censure injustice fearing that they may be the victims of it and not because they are afraid of committing it.

—Plato, *The Republic*

There is a point beyond which even justice becomes unjust.

—Sophocles, *Electra*

It's preferable to be wronged than to wrong.

—Socrates, fragment

Be brave, justice always prevails!

—Euripides

What is lawful is not binding only on some and not binding on others. Lawfulness extends everywhere, through the wide-ruling air and the boundless light of the sky.

—**Empedocles, fragment**

All souls are immortal, but the souls of the virtuous are both immortal and divine.

—**Socrates, fragment**

The manner by which the masses can see the beauty of justice is to teach them, by simple means, the results of injustice.

—**Euripides**

Justice tamed everything that's human.

—**Plato,** *Laws*

When strength is yoked with justice,
where is a mightier pair than they?

—**Aeschylus, fragment**

Justice brings much pleasure to the soul because living without having anything to fear or be ashamed of is a pleasure and satisfaction in life.

—**Diogenes of Sinope**

Time alone reveals the just man; but you might discern a bad man in a single day.

—**Sophocles,** *Oedipus at Colonus*

A judge rules the soul with the soul.

—**Plato,** *The Republic*

An unjust deed doesn't escape the gods' attention.

—**Plato,** *Laws*

What the judge does is to restore equality.

—**Aristotle,** *Ethics*

Practice justice in word and deed, and do not get in the habit of acting thoughtlessly about anything.

—**Pythagoras**

Justice will overtake fabricators of lies and false witnesses.

—**Heraclitus, fragments**

To do injustice is the greatest of all evils.

—**Plato,** *Gorgias*

LEADERSHIP

An army of deer led by a lion is more to be feared than an army of lions led by a deer.

—**Philip II, king of Macedonia**

There is no greater proof of the abilities of a general than to investigate, with the utmost care, into the character and natural abilities of his opponent.

—**Polybius,** *Histories*

Be slow in action and when you act be steady.

—**Bias of Priene, fragment**

The noble part of the soul, not the illogical, must lead the soul.

—**Aristotle,** *Politics*

A good general not only sees the way to victory; he also knows when victory is impossible.

—**Polybius,** *Histories*

What a great statesman must be most anxious to produce is a certain moral character in his fellow citizens, namely a disposition to virtue and the performance of virtuous actions.

—**Aristotle,** *Ethics*

It is impossible to know fully any man's character, will, or judgment, until he has been proved by the test of rule and law-giving.

—**Sophocles,** *Antigone*

On him who wields power gently, the god looks favorably from afar.

—**Aeschylus,** *Agamemnon*

He who is to be a good ruler must have first been ruled.

—**Aristotle,** *Politics*

A monarch, when he decides to change the moral habits of a State, needs no great efforts nor a vast length of time, but what he does need is to lead the way himself first along the desired path, whether it be to urge the citizens towards virtue's practices or the contrary; by his personal example he should first trace out the right lines, giving praise and honor to these things, blame to those, and degrading the disobedient according to their several deeds.

—**Plato,** *Laws*

LICENTIOUSNESS

He who desires a shameful act, will carry it out first chance he gets.

—**Cleanthes, fragment**

Even if it feels pleasant, a shameful life remains disgraceful.

—**Menander, fragment**

It is hard to find in excessive persons a decent habit, as is in sick persons a healthy one.

  —**Plato**

Pursue the enjoyments which are of good repute; for pleasure attended by honor is the best thing in the world, but pleasure without honor is the worst.

  —**Isocrates, letter to Demonicus**

If you feel that a suitable occasion has arisen to [commit a sin], be careful not to allow its enticement, and sweetness, and attractiveness, to overcome you; but set over against all this the thought, how much better is the consciousness of having won a victory over it.

  —**Epictetus,** *Enchiridion*

It is hard to contend against one's heart's desire; for whatever it wishes to have it buys at the cost of the soul.

  —**Heraclitus, fragment**

What man that is the slave of his pleasures is not in an evil plight body and soul alike?

  —**Xenophon,** *Memorabilia*

MATERIALISM

External goods, being like a collection of tools each useful for some purpose, have a limit: one can have too many of them, and that is bound to be of no benefit, or even a positive injury, to their possessors.

—**Aristotle,** *Politics*

Know not to revere human things too much.

—**Aeschylus, fragment**

To each man there comes just so much happiness as he has of virtue and of practical wisdom, and performs actions dependent thereon. God Himself is an indication of the truth of this. He is blessed and happy not on account of any of the external goods but because of Himself and what He is by His own nature.

—**Aristotle,** *Politics*

How many things there are which I do not need!

—**Socrates, upon seeing an auction at the market-place, as quoted by Diogenes Laërtius in** *Lives of Eminent Philosophers*

It is not by means of external goods that men acquire and keep the virtues but the other way around.

—**Aristotle,** *Politics*

MODERATION

Nothing in excess.

—Thales of Miletus, fragment

Profligacy [means] choosing harmful and base pleasures and enjoyments, and thinking that the happiest people are those who pass their lives in pleasures of that kind, and being fond of laughter and mockery and jokes and levity in words and deeds. Profligacy is accompanied by disorder, shamelessness, irregularity, luxury, slackness, carelessness, negligence, remissness.

—Aristotle, *Virtues and Vices*

Moderation, the noblest gift of Heaven.

—Euripides, *Medea*

Self-control [is the] ability to restrain desire by reason when it is set on base enjoyments and pleasures, and to be resolute, and [have] readiness to endure natural want and pain.

—Aristotle, *Virtues and Vices*

If possible avoid drinking-parties altogether, but if ever occasion arises when you must be present, rise and take your leave before you become intoxicated; for when the mind is impaired by wine it is like chariots which have lost their drivers; for just as these plunge along in wild disorder when they miss the hands which should guide them, so the soul stumbles again and again when the intellect is impaired.

—Isocrates, letter to Demonicus

Everyone enjoys tasty food and wine and sex in some degree, but not everyone to the right degree.

—Aristotle, *Ethics*

One must choose in all things a mean just and good.

—Pythagoras

To [be uncontrolled is] to choose the enjoyment of pleasures when reason would restrain, and although one believes that it would be better not to participate in them, to participate in them all the same, and while thinking one ought to do fine and expedient things yet to abstain from them for the sake of one's pleasures. The concomitants of uncontrol are softness and negligence and in general the same as those of profligacy.

—Aristotle, *Virtues and Vices*

Practice restraint over the following: appetite, first, as well as sleep, lust, and anger.

—Pythagoras

The man who gets angry at the right things and with the right people, and also in the right way and at the right time and for the right length of time is commended; so this person will be patient, inasmuch as patience is commendable, because a patient person tends to be unperturbed and not carried away by his feelings, but indignant only in the way and on the grounds and for the length of time that his principle prescribes.

—**Aristotle,** *Ethics*

Do not spend in excess like one who is careless of what is good, nor be miserly; the mean is best in every case.

—**Pythagoras**

Temperance is a mean with regard to pleasures.

—**Aristotle,** *Ethics*

Contempt of pleasure . . .

—**King Agesilaus of Sparta, upon being asked what good had Lycurgus' laws brought to Sparta, as quoted in Plutarch's** *Saying of Spartans*

MODESTY

Even if you are all alone, speak and do no evil and learn to be first ashamed of your own self and then of what others may say of you.

—**Democritus**

Respect yourself and you will feel ashamed of no one.

    —Theophrastos

You will be respected by everyone if you first start respecting yourself.

    —Mousonios, fragment

Conceit is a trait of an immoral person while modesty of a serious one.

    —Filo, fragment

In your conversation avoid making mention at great length and excessively of your own deeds or dangers, because it is not as pleasant for others to hear about your adventures, as it is for you to call to mind your own dangers.

    —Epictetus, *Enchiridion*

Among all human beings, first respect yourself.

    —Pythagoras

Wherever there is fear there exists respect.

    —Plutarch

In all things resolve to act as though the whole world would see what you do; for even if you conceal your deeds for the moment, later you will be found out. But most of all will you have the respect of men, if you are seen to avoid doing things which you would blame others for doing.

—Isocrates, letter to Demonicus

Verily nature has . . . given me a sense of shame, and frequently blush, when I feel that I am saying something disgraceful. It is this emotion which does not allow me to lay down pleasure as the good and end of life.

—Epictetus, fragments

The greatest treasure you can leave your children is a sense of modesty and the advice to follow virtuous persons.

—Theognis

Avoid raising a laugh, for this is a kind of behavior that slips easily into vulgarity, and at the same time is calculated to lessen the respect which your neighbors have of you.

—Epictetus, *Enchiridion*

Shame is not the emotion of a good man, if it is felt for doing bad actions, because such actions ought not to be done (and it makes no difference whether the things done are really shameful or are only thought to be so; they should not be done in either case); so the emotion ought not to be felt.

—Aristotle, *Ethics*

It is dangerous . . . to lapse into foul language. When, therefore, anything of the sort occurs, if the occasion be suitable, go even so far as to reprove the person who has made such a lapse; if, however, the occasion does not arise, at all events show by keeping silence, and blushing, and frowning, that you are displeased by what has been said.

—**Epictetus,** *Enchiridion*

PATRIOTISM

Compared with your mother and father and all the rest of your ancestors your country is something far more precious, more venerable, more sacred, and held in greater honor both among gods and among all reasonable men.

—**Plato,** *Crito*

Without a sign his sword the brave man draws,
And asks no omen but his country's cause.

—**Homer,** *The Iliad*

If [your country] leads you out to war, to be wounded or killed, you must comply, and it is just that this should be so—you must not give way or retreat or abandon your position.

—**Plato,** *Crito*

What a fine thing it is to refuse to sell your country!

—Demosthenes, *Speeches*

PROCRASTINATION

Do not put your work off till tomorrow and the day after; for a sluggish worker does not fill his barn, nor one who puts off his work: Industry makes work go well, but a man who puts off work is always at hand-grips with ruin.

—Hesiod, *Works and Days*

SELFISHNESS AND SELF-ABSORPTION

For just as poets love their own works, and fathers their own children, in the same way those who have created a fortune value their money, not merely for its uses, like other persons, but because it is their own production. This makes them moreover disagreeable companions, because they will praise nothing but riches.

—Plato, *The Republic*

The cause of all sins in every case lies in the person's excessive love of self.

—**Plato,** *Laws*

It is surely no accident that every man has affection for himself: nature meant this to be so. Selfishness is condemned, and justly, but selfishness is not simply to be fond of oneself, but to be excessively fond.

—**Aristotle,** *Politics*

SELF-KNOWLEDGE

Know thyself.

—**Inscription at the Oracle of Apollo at Delphi**

The unexamined life is not worth living.

—**Socrates, as quoted in Plato's** *Apology*

It is the part of an uneducated person to blame others where he himself fares ill; to blame himself is the part of one whose education has begun; to blame neither another nor his own self is the part of one whose education is already complete.

—**Epictetus,** *Enchiridion*

To win over your bad self is the grandest and foremost of victories.

—**Plato**

To deceive yourself and believe that which you don't know to, indeed, know is borderline madness.

—Socrates

Knowing yourself is the beginning of all wisdom.

—Aristotle

Getting to know yourself is extremely difficult.

—Thales of Miletus, fragment

I investigate not [mythical creatures] but myself, to know whether I am a monster more complicated and more furious than Typhon* or a gentler and simpler creature, to whom a divine and quiet lot is given by nature.

—Socrates, as quoted in Plato's *Phaedrus*

Don't attempt to heal others when you yourself are full of wounds.

—Euripides

Generally, we're all wise when advising others but we fail to see that we also err.

—Socrates

* A monster in Greek mythology, often described as a destructive hurricane or a fire-breathing giant. Typhon is depicted as having 100 heads, frightening eyes, and producing terrible voices. Typhon sought sovereignty over gods and men, but, after a fierce struggle, was finally subdued by Zeus with a thunderbolt.

Learn what it is to be human and you'll be a better human.

    —Antiphanes, fragment

You will become a teacher of yourself when for the same things that you blame others, you also blame yourself.

    —Diogenes of Sinope, fragment

Self-knowledge is observation of your actions and knowing the right thing to do at any given moment.

    —Menander, fragment

I am certainly wiser than this man. It is only too likely that neither of us has any knowledge to boast of; but he thinks that he knows something which he does not know, whereas I am quite conscious of my ignorance. At any rate it seems that I am wiser than he is to this small extent, that I do not think that I know what I do not know.

    —Socrates, as quoted in Plato's *Apology*

Don't try to cover your mistakes with false words. Rather, correct your mistakes with examination.

    —Pythagoras, fragment

There's a victory and defeat—the first and best of victories, the lowest and worst of defeats—which each man gains or sustains at the hands not of another, but of himself.

    —Plato, *Protagoras*

Because you are a mortal, think as a mortal.

  —Menander, fragment

Do not let sleep close your tired eyes until you have three times gone over the events of the day. "What did I do wrong? What did I accomplish? What did I fail to do that I should have done?" Starting from the beginning, go through to the end. Then reproach yourself for the things you did wrong, and take pleasure in the good things you did.

  —Pythagoras

SELF-RESTRAINT

Avoid all wrath.

  —Pythagoras

I have often repented speaking, but never of holding my tongue.

  —Xenocrates, fragment

Self-control is the chief element in self-respect and self-respect is the chief element in courage.

  —Thucydides, *The History of the Peloponnesean War*

Make self-control a habit.

—**Pythagoras**

SLANDER

A man slandered is doubly injured—first by him who utters the calumny, and then by him who believes it.

—**Herodotus**, *Histories*

Guard yourself against accusations, even if they are false; for the multitude are ignorant of the truth and look only to reputation.

—**Isocrates, letter to Demonicus**

He who readily accepts slanders as truth has either an evil character or a child's ability to judge.

—**Menander, fragment**

You should punish in the same manner those who commit crimes with those who accuse falsely.

—**Thucydides**

Don't you know that silence supports the accuser's charge?

—**Sophocles**, *The Women of Trachis*

A gen'rous heart repairs a sland'rous tongue.
>—Homer, *The Odyssey*

Now I see that going out into the testing ground of men it is the tongue and not the deed that wins the day.
>—Sophocles, *Philoctetes*

TRUTH AND LYING

Throughout your life choose truth and your words will be more believable than other people's oaths.
>—Isocrates, *letter to Nicocles*

You should not honor men more than truth.
>—Plato, *The Republic*

Plato is dear to me, yet dearer is truth.
>—Aristotle

False words are not only evil in themselves, but they infect the soul with evil.
>—Socrates

The greatest enemy of all is considered he who tells the truth.

—Plato, *The Republic*

Simple is the speech of truth.

—Aeschylus, fragment, *Oplon Krisis*

It is unjust to be upset with him who tells the truth.

—Plato, *The Republic*

Lying is meanness and truth bravery.

—Appolonius, fragment

No lie ever reaches old age.

—Sophocles, fragment

Nobody likes the bringer of bad news.

—Sophocles, *Antigone*

I have never wished to cater to the crowd; for what I know they do not approve, and what they approve I do not know.

—Epicurus, fragment

The truth is always the strongest argument.

—Sophocles, *Phaedra*

I am bound to tell what I am told, but not in every case to believe it.

—Herodotus, *Histories*

Time will reveal everything. It is a babbler and speaks even when not asked.

—Euripides, fragment

UNGRATEFULNESS

He who, when benefited by a friend or enemy does not return the favor, is unfair.

—Xenophon, *Memorabilia*

VIOLENCE

Deliberate violence is more to be quenched than a fire.

—Heraclitus, fragment

Violence is accompanied by hate and danger. Yet, you can achieve the same results using persuasion and friendliness minus the danger.

—Xenophon, *Memorabilia*

Force has no place where there is need of skill.

> —**Herodotus,** *Histories*

Discordance is evil. Harmony is virtue.

> —**Plato, fragment**

VIRTUE AND BECOMING VIRTUOUS

Like a statue that is fixed steadily on its base, the virtuous man ought to be stable in character.

> —**Socrates**

Before virtue, Gods have placed sweat.

> —**Hesiod**

He who in his own house is virtuous will also be just in civic affairs.

> —**Sophocles, fragment**

All of the earth's gold is not worth virtue.

> —**Plato**

Discourse on virtue and they pass by in droves; whistle and dance, and you've got an audience.

> —**Diogenes of Sinope, fragment**

Virtue in itself is not enough; there must also be the power to translate it into action.

—**Aristotle,** *Politics*

Greatness of spirit [is] to bear finely both good fortune and bad, honor and disgrace, and not to think highly of luxury or attention or power or victories in contests, and to possess a certain depth and magnitude of spirit. He who values life highly and who is fond of life is not great-spirited. The great-spirited man is simple and noble in character, able to bear injustice and not revengeful. Greatness of spirit is accompanied by simplicity and sincerity.

—**Aristotle,** *Virtues and Vices*

Fly from the company of the wicked—fly and turn not back.

—**Plato,** *Protagoras*

Moral good is a practical stimulus; it is no sooner seen than it inspires an impulse to practice.

—**Pericles, as quoted in Plutarch's** *Life of Pericles*

Each virtue makes men disdainful of things irrationally deemed great: For example, courage makes a man disdainful of dangers, for he thinks that to consider danger a great matter is a disgraceful thing, and that numbers are not always formidable; and the sober-minded man disdains great and numerous pleasures, and the liberal man wealth.

—**Aristotle,** *Eudemian Ethics*

It is very difficult to become a virtuous man.

—**Plato**, *Protagoras*

It is a greater sin to disregard virtue while knowing what virtue is, than never to have known any virtue at all.

—**Xenophon**

It's shameful to recognize virtue in others while we are conquered by vices.

—**Bias of Priene**

Living would be worthless if the gods delighted in receiving offerings from evil persons rather than from the virtuous.

—**Xenophon**

Zeus sent man both justice and a sense of shame.

—**Plato**, *Protagoras*

Goodness [is] to do good to the deserving and love the good and hate the wicked, and not to be eager to inflict punishment or take vengeance, but [be] gracious and kindly and forgiving. Goodness is accompanied by honesty, reasonableness, kindness, hopefulness, and also by such traits as love of home and of friends and comrades and guests, and of one's fellow-men, and love of what is noble.

—**Aristotle**, *Virtues and Vices*

Virtuous men have never destroyed a state.

    —Theognis

Nothing goes right for the man who is bereft of virtue.

    —Xenophon, fragment

The virtuous man has a steadfast character and opinions and he is daring whether in pleasant or unpleasant situations.

    —Theognis

Protecting virtue is harder than acquiring it.

    —Demosthenes

A person's value doesn't depend on his qualities but on the way he uses them.

    —Aristotle, fragment

Even after death, our virtue is not lost.

    —Euripides

Virtue is acquired with toil.

    —Hesiod

Cities must be beautified not with beautiful buildings but with the virtues of their citizens.

    —Zeno of Elea

A virtuous man cannot hate another virtuous man.

> —Menander

The more you practice virtue the easier to practice it becomes.

> —Euripides

Pleasures are temporary but virtues immortal.

> —Periander

All the virtues are cultivated by studying and learning.

> —Xenophon

The most unholy and savage animal is a human being without virtue.

> —Aristotle, *Laws*

In order to have a good future, you must pay attention to the present. You should seek to be remembered for your virtue rather than your physical attributes.

> —Isocrates, fragment

Virtue in action is more important than rhetoric or preaching.

> —Antisthenes, fragment

We are each a teacher of virtue, each one of us as we possibly can.

> —Plato, *Protagoras*

The components of virtue are justice, courage, self-control, magnificence, magnanimity, liberality, gentleness, practical and speculative wisdom.

—**Aristotle,** *Rhetoric*

To become virtuous is difficult but possible.

—**Plato,** *Protagoras*

In order to be effective you need not only virtue but also mental strength.

—**Aristotle,** *Politics*

If you wish to become virtuous, first acknowledge that you are not.

—**Epictetus, fragment**

Righteousness [is] to be ready to distribute according to desert, and to preserve ancestral customs and institutions and the established laws, and to tell the truth when interest is at stake, and to keep agreements. First among the claims of righteousness are our duties to the gods, then our duties to the spirits, then those to country and parents, then those to the departed; and among these claims is piety, which is either a part of righteousness or a concomitant of it. Righteousness is also accompanied by holiness and truth and loyalty and hatred of wickedness.

—**Aristotle,** *Virtues and Vices*

Whatever moral rules you have deliberately proposed to yourself abide by them as if they were laws, and as if you would be guilty of impiety by violating any of them. Don't regard what anyone says of you, for this, after all, is no concern of yours.

—Epictetus, *Enchiridion*

Virtue isn't not wronging others but not *wishing* to wrong others.

—Democritus, fragment

Reverence does not die with mortals, nor does it perish whether they live or die.

—Sophocles, *Philoctetes*

The life which is best for men, both separately, as individuals, and in the mass, as states, is the life which has virtue sufficiently supported by material resources to facilitate participation in the actions that virtue calls for.

—Aristotle, *Politics*

You are mistaken, my friend, if you think that a man who is worth anything ought to spend his time weighing up the prospects of life and death. He has only one thing to consider in performing any action; that is, whether he is acting justly or unjustly, like a good man or a bad one.

—Socrates, as quoted in Plato's *Apology*

Cities ought not to be fortified with stones and timbers, but with the strong virtues of their inhabitants.

> —Agesilaus II, as quoted in Plutarch's *Sayings of Spartans*

Virtue consists more in doing good than in receiving it, and more in doing fine actions than in refraining from disgraceful ones.

> —Aristotle, *Ethics*

Do nothing shameful in private or with another.

> —Pythagoras

Goodness is an enduring quality.

> —Aristotle, *Ethics*

THE WISE

He who can properly summarize many ideas in a brief statement, is a wise man.

> —Euripides

Wise men take opportunities, and do not overstep their fate to get other pleasures.

> —Euripides, *Iphigenia in Tauris*

Appearances to the mind are of four kinds. Things either are what they appear to be; or they neither are, nor appear to be; or they are, and do not appear to be; or they are not, and yet appear to be. Rightly to aim in all these cases is the wise man's task.

—Epictetus, *Discourses*

Justice inclines her scales so that wisdom comes at the price of suffering.

—Aeschylus, *Agamemnon*

For never, never, wicked man was wise.

—Homer, *The Odyssey*

A wise man does not chatter with one whose mind is sick.

—Sophocles, *The Women of Trachis*

A wise man's country [is] the world.

—Aristippus, as quoted by Diogenes Laërtius in *Lives of Eminent Philosophers*

Whenever a person strives, by the help of dialectic, to start in pursuit of every reality by a simple process of reason, independent of all sensuous information—never flinching, until by an act of the pure intelligence he has grasped the real nature of good—he arrives at the very end of the intellectual world.

—Plato, *The Republic*

The most hateful human misfortune is for a wise man to have no influence.

—**Herodotus,** *Histories*

WORK AND LAZINESS

Laziness is the source of many evils.

—**Menander**

Work is not a shame. Laziness is a shame.

—**Hesiod**

Hunger is an altogether fit companion for the idle man.

—**Hesiod,** *Works and Days*

If men are given food, but no chastisement nor any work, they become insolent.

—**Aristotle,** *Economics*

You will not achieve happiness if you don't work hard; and it's a shame not to want to work hard.

—**Euripides**

64

Both gods and men are angry with a man who lives idle, for in nature he is like the stingless drones who waste the labor of the bees, eating without working; but let it be your care to order your work properly, that in the right season your barns may be full of victual. Through work men grow rich in flocks and substance.

—Hesiod, *Works and Days*

If you wish to be a good reader, read; if you wish to be a good writer, write.

—Epictetus, *Discourses*

Laziness is the mother of all evils.

—Sophocles

GOD AND RELIGION

GOD

Mortals consider that the gods are born, and that they have clothes and speech and bodies like their own. . . . The Ethiopians say that their gods are snub-nosed and black, the Thracians that theirs have light blue eyes and red hair. . . . But if cattle and horses or lions had hands, or were able to draw with their hands and do the works that men can do, horses would draw the forms of the gods like horses, and cattle like cattle, and they would make their bodies such as they each had themselves. . . . [There is] one God, greatest among gods and men, in no way similar to mortals either in body or in thought.

—Xenophanes, as quoted by Clement

Remember that you are an actor in a play, the character of which is determined by the Playwright: If He wishes the play to be short, it is short; if long, it is long; if He wishes you to play the part of a beggar, remember to act even this role adroitly; and so if your role be that of a cripple, an official, or a layman. For this is your business, to play admirably the role assigned you; but the selection of that role is Another's.

—Epictetus, *Enchiridion*

First of all, then, show devotion to the gods, not merely by doing sacrifice, but also by keeping your vows; for the former is but evidence of a material prosperity, whereas the latter is proof of a noble character.

—Isocrates, letter to Demonicus

No human being is an orphan, but all men have ever and constantly the Father, who cares for them.

—Epictetus, *Discourses*

In the worship of the gods, follow the example of your ancestors, but believe that the noblest sacrifice and the greatest devotion is to show yourself in the highest degree a good and just man.

—Isocrates, letter to Nicocles

When you come into the presence of some prominent man, remember that Another looks from above on what is taking place, and that you must please Him rather than this man.

—Epictetus, *Discourses*

Always [God] remains in the same place, moving not at all; nor is it fitting for Him to go to different places at different times, but without toil He shakes all things by the thought of his mind.

  —Xenophanes, as quoted in Simplicius' *Physics*

God has brought man into the world to be a spectator of Himself and of His works, and not merely a spectator, but also an interpreter.

  —Epictetus, *Discourses*

To God all things are beautiful and good and just, but men have supposed some things to be unjust, others just.

  —Heraclitus, as quoted in Porphyrius' *Iliadem*

You are bearing God about with you, you poor wretch, and know it not! Do you suppose I am speaking of some external God, made of silver or gold? It is within yourself that you bear Him, and do not perceive that you are defiling Him with impure thoughts and filthy actions.

  —Epictetus, *Discourses*

For the lips of Zeus do not know how to lie, but bring to fulfillment every word.

  —Aeschylus, *Prometheus Bound*

Each man's life is a kind of campaign, and a long and complicated one at that. You have to maintain the character of a soldier, and do each separate act at the bidding of the General.

—Epictetus, *Discourses*

Nothing can harm a good man either in life or after death and his fortunes are not a matter of indifference to the gods.

—Socrates, *Apology*

When God throws, the dice are loaded.

—Ancient Greek proverb

The most beautiful ape is ugly when compared to a human. The wisest human will seem like an ape when compared to a god with respect to wisdom, beauty, and everything else.

—Heraclitus, fragments

They also say that God is an animal immortal, rational, perfect, and intellectual in His happiness, unsusceptible of any kind of evil, having a foreknowledge of the universe and of all that is in the universe; however, that He has not the figure of a man; and that He is the creator of the universe, and as it were the Father of all things in common, and that a portion of Him pervades everything.

—Zeno of Elea, fragment

You travel to Olympia to behold the work of Pheidias,* and each

* The famous gold and ivory statue of Zeus

of you regards it as a misfortune to die without seeing such sights; yet when there is no need to travel at all, but where Zeus is already, and is present in His works, will you not yearn to behold these works and know them?

—Epictetus *Discourses*

God is day and night, winter and summer, war and peace, surfeit and hunger.

—Heraclitus, fragment

PRAYER AND HOPE

Being mortal, never pray for an untroubled life. Rather, ask the gods to give you an enduring heart.

—Menander, fragment

For this is the mark of a wise and upright man,
not to rail against the gods in misfortune.

—Aeschylus, fragment

One must endure what the god gives, whatever it is.

—Euripides, *Alcestis*

Exiles feed on hope.

> —Aeschylus, *Agamemnon*

Youth is easily deceived because it is quick to hope.

> —Aristotle, *Rhetoric*

If you wish the gods to be propitious to you, you must honor the gods.

> —Xenophon, *Memorabilia*

What atonement is there for blood spilt upon the earth?

> —Aeschylus, *The Libation Bearers*

SOUL

You are a little soul, carrying around a corpse.

> —Epictetus, fragments

When death comes to a man, the mortal part of him dies, but the undying part retires at the approach of death and escapes unharmed and indestructible.

> —Socrates, as quoted in Plato's *Phaedo*

You would not find out the boundaries of soul, even by traveling along every path: so deep a measure does it have.

> —Heraclitus, as quoted by Diogenes Laërtius in *Lives of Eminent Philosophers*

How prophetic the soul is, my friend!

> —Socrates, as quoted in Plato's *Phaedrus*

To go to the world below, having a soul which is like a vessel full of injustice, is the last and worst of all the evils.

> —Plato, *Gorgias*

And some say that [the soul] is intermingled in the universe, for which reason, perhaps, Thales also thought that all things are full of gods.

> —Aristotle, *On the Soul*

The functions of a soul are the exercise of choice, of refusal, of desire, of aversion, of preparation, of purpose, and of assent.

> —Epictetus, *Discourses*

Eyes and ears are poor witnesses to people if they have uncultured souls.

> —Heraclitus, fragments

The mind [is] the pilot of the soul.

> —Socrates, as quoted in Plato's *Phaedrus*

If thinking is like perceiving, it must be either a process in which the soul is acted upon by what is capable of being thought, or a process different from but analogous to that. The thinking part of the soul must therefore be, while impassable, capable of receiving the form of an object; that is, must be potentially identical in character with its object without being the object. Mind must be related to what is thinkable, as sense is to what is sensible.

—**Aristotle,** *On the Soul*

A soul that is kind and intends justice discovers more than any sophist.

—**Sophocles**

THANKSGIVING

From everything that happens in the universe it is easy for a man to find occasion to praise providence, if he has within himself these two qualities: the faculty of taking a comprehensive view of what has happened in each individual instance, and the sense of gratitude.

—**Epictetus,** *Discourses*

Why, what else can I, a lame old man, do but sing hymns to God? If, indeed, I were a nightingale, I should be singing as a nightingale;

if a swan, as a swan. But as it is, I am a rational being, therefore I must be singing hymns of praise to God.

—Epictetus, *Discourses*

Now, when we have been invited to a banquet, we take what is set before us; and if a person should bid his host to set before him fish or cakes, he would be regarded as eccentric. Yet in the world at large we ask the gods for things which they do not give us, and that too when there are many things which they actually have given us.

—Epictetus, fragments

HUMANITY

ADVICE

Whenever you purpose to consult with anyone about your affairs, first observe how he has managed his own; for he who has shown poor judgment in conducting his own business will never give wise counsel about the business of others.

> —Isocrates, letter to Demonicus

No enemy is more damaging than bad advice.

> —Sophocles, *Electra*

A fool you can neither persuade nor break.

> —Epictetus, *Discourses,*

Evil counsel travels fast.

> —Sophocles, fragment

To think well and to consent to obey someone giving good advice are the same thing.

  —Herodotus, *Histories*

To me no profitable speech sounds ill.

  —Sophocles, *Electra*

AGING AND OLD AGE

Nobody loves life like him who's growing old.

  —Sophocles, *Acrisius*

He who is of a calm and happy nature will hardly feel the pressure of age and time, but to him who is of an opposite disposition, youth and age are equally a heavy burden.

  —Plato, *The Republic*

Seek the friendship of the elderly.

  —Strabo, fragment

Old age and the passage of time teach us everything.

  —Sophocles, fragment

We must respect the elderly with words and actions.

    —**Plato**

When young, seek to listen to elders' conversations.

    —**Strabo, fragment**

A man growing old becomes a child again.

    —**Sophocles**

Time purges all things, aging with them.

    —**Aeschylus,** *Eumenides*

There is no such thing as the old age of the wise.

    —**Sophocles**

It is good even for old men to learn wisdom.

    —**Aeschylus, fragment**

In particular I may mention Sophocles the poet, who was once asked in my presence, "How do you feel about love, Sophocles? Are you still capable of it?" to which he replied, "Hush! if you please: To my great delight I have escaped from it, and feel as if I had escaped from a frantic and savage master." I thought then, as I do now, that he spoke wisely. For unquestionably old age brings us profound repose and freedom from this and other passions.

    —**Plato,** *The Republic*

BEAUTY AND UGLINESS

What is beautiful is good and he who is good will soon also be beautiful.

>   —**Sappho, fragment**

Beauty of soul is not so easy to see as beauty of body.

>   —**Aristotle,** *Politics*

Modesty is the citadel of beauty.

>   —**Menander**

In youth and beauty wisdom is but rare!

>   —**Homer,** *The Odyssey*

It seems to me that whatever else is beautiful apart from absolute beauty is beautiful because it partakes of that absolute beauty, and for no other reason.

>   —**Plato,** *Phaedo*

She moves a goddess, and she looks a queen.

>   —**Homer,** *The Iliad*

COMPETITION

Wherever there is competition, there's victory.

—**Aristotle**

Always excel and be better than the rest.

—**Homer**

So you wish to conquer in the Olympic games, my friend? And I too, by the Gods, and a fine thing it would be! But first mark the conditions and the consequences, and then set to work. You will have to put yourself under discipline; to eat by rule, to avoid cakes and sweetmeats; to take exercise at the appointed hour whether you like it or not, in cold and heat; to abstain from cold drinks and from wine at your will; in a word, to give yourself over to the trainer as to a physician. Then in the conflict itself you are likely enough to dislocate your wrist or twist your ankle, to swallow a great deal of dust, or to be severely thrashed, and, after all these things, to be defeated.

—**Epictetus,** *Enchiridion*

The first in glory, as the first in place.

—**Homer,** *The Odyssey*

In the race for wealth, a neighbor tries to outdo his neighbor, but this strife is good for men. For the potter envies potter, and the carpenter the carpenter, and the beggar rivals the beggar, and the singer the singer.

—**Hesiod,** *Works and Days*

COOPERATION

Think not that thy word and thine alone must be right.

—Sophocles, *Antigone*

One hand washes the other.

—Menander

In regard to a just deed, it is unreasonable for two people to argue, but reasonable to jump to action.

—Sophocles, *Electra*

No treaty is ever an impediment to a cheat.

—Sophocles, fragment

DEATH

Whom the gods love, dies young.

—Menander, *Dis Exapaton*

Death is an evil; the gods have so decided. Had death been good, gods would also die.

—Sappho, fragment

Never in any case say *I have lost* such a thing, but *I have returned it*. Is your child dead? It is a return. Is your wife dead? It is a return.
>—Epictetus, *Enchiridion*

Who dies in youth and vigor, dies the best.
>—Homer, *The Iliad*

It is not safe to honor with hymns and praises those still living, before they have traversed the whole of life and reached a noble end.
>—Plato, *Laws*

To fear death, my friends, is only to think ourselves wise, without being wise: for it is to think that we know what we do not know. For anything that men can tell, death may be the greatest good that can happen to them: but they fear it as if they knew quite well that it was the greatest of evils. And what is this but that shameful ignorance of thinking that we know what we do not know?
>—Socrates, as quoted in Plato's *Apology*

If you wish your children, and your wife, and your friends to live for ever, you are stupid; for you wish to be in control of things which you cannot, you wish for things that belong to others to be your own.
>—Epictetus, *Enchiridion*

As for our mortal life, this is not the first time that I have thought it to be a shadow, and I would say without any fear that those mortals who seem to be clever and workers-up of polished speeches are guilty of the greatest folly. For no mortal ever attains to blessedness. One may be luckier than another when wealth flows his way, but blessed never.

—Euripides, *Medea*

Death is a debt which all of us must pay.

—Sophocles, *Electra*

Of all the gods, Death only craves not gifts:
Nor sacrifice, nor yet drink-offering poured
Avails; no altars hath he, nor is soothed
By hymns of praise. From him alone of all
The powers of heaven Persuasion holds aloof.

—Aeschylus, fragment

The paltry body must be separated from the bit of spirit, either now or later, just as it existed apart from it before. Why are you grieved, then, if it be separated now? For if it be not separated now, it will be later.

—Epictetus, *Discourses*

Death, the most dreaded of all evils, is therefore of no concern to us; for while we exist death is not present, and when death is present we no longer exist.

—Epicurus, letter to Menoeceus

Immortal mortals, mortal immortals, one living the others' death and dying the others' life.

> —Heraclitus, fragment

I am not eternal, but a man; a part of the whole, as an hour is part of a day. I must come on as the hour and like an hour pass away.

> —Epictetus, *Discourses*

Old men's prayers for death are lying prayers,
in which they abuse old age and long extent of life.
But when death draws near, not one is willing to die,
and age no longer is a burden to them.

> —Euripides, *Alcestis*

[God] has thrown open the door and says to you, "Go." Where? To nothing you need to fear, but back to that from which you came, to what is friendly and akin to you, to the physical elements. What there was of fire in you shall pass into fire, what there was of earth into earth, what there was of spirit into spirit, what there was of water, into water.

> —Epictetus, *Discourses*

Not even old age knows how to love death.

> —Sophocles, fragment

It is not the things themselves that disturb men, but their judgments about these things. For example, death is nothing dreadful, or else Socrates too would have thought so, but the judgment that death is dreadful, this is the dreadful thing.

—**Epictetus,** *Enchiridion*

Death is not the worst evil, but rather when we wish to die and cannot.

—**Sophocles,** *Electra*

Who knows, life may be that which men call death,
And death what men call life.

—**Euripides, fragments**

When a man deems life at any price to be a good thing, then also he does not honor, but dishonor, to his soul; for he yields to the imagination of his soul that the conditions in Hades are altogether evil, instead of opposing it, by teaching and convincing his soul that, for all it knows, we may find, on the contrary, our greatest blessings in the realm of the gods below.

—**Plato,** *Laws*

'T is true,' t is certain; man though dead retains
Part of himself: The immortal mind remains.

—**Homer,** *The Iliad*

DIVORCE AND INFIDELITY

As for extramarital intercourse, it should, in general, be a disgrace to be detected in intimacy of any kind whatever, so long as one is a husband and so addressed.

—**Aristotle,** *Politics*

A Roman divorced from his wife, being highly blamed by his friends, who demanded, "Was she not chaste? Was she not fair? Was she not fruitful?" holding out his shoe, asked them whether it was not new and well made. "Yet," added he, "none of you can tell where it pinches me."

—**Plutarch,** *Lives*

A man does wrong to his wife when he associates with other women.

—**Aristotle,** *Economics*

ENEMIES

Pay attention to your enemies because they are the first to discover your mistakes.

—**Antisthenes, fragment**

The practical measures that we take are always based on the assumption that our enemies are not unintelligent.

—**Archidamus III, king of Sparta**

It will be impossible to defeat the enemies outside the city unless you defeat the enemies within it.

—**Demosthenes,** *Philippic*

The laughter of one's enemies is unendurable.

—**Euripides,** *Medea*

But this is a true saying among men: the gifts of enemies are no gifts and profitless.

—**Sophocles,** *Ajax*

Men are not our friends and our foes by natural generation: they are made such by their own actions; and the law gives us freedom to chastise as enemies those whose acts are hostile.

—**Demosthenes,** *Speeches*

ENVY

Few men have the natural strength to honor a friend's success without envy. . . . I well know that mirror of friendship, shadow of a shade.

—Aeschylus, *Agamemnon*

Admit to your companionship, not those alone who show distress at your reverses, but those also who show no envy at your good fortune; for there are many who sympathize with their friends in adversity, but envy them in prosperity.

—Isocrates, letter to Demonicus

Envy consists in being annoyed at prosperity more often than one ought to be, for the envious are annoyed by the prosperity even of those who deserve to prosper; the opposite character is less definitely named, but it is the man that goes too far in not being annoyed even at the prosperity of the undeserving, and is easy going, as gluttons are in regard to food, whereas his opposite is difficult-tempered in respect of jealousy.

—Aristotle, *Eudemian Ethics*

FAILURE

A bad beginning makes a bad ending.

> **—Euripides, fragment**

Even from the first it is meek to seek the impossible.

> **—Sophocles,** *Antigone*

FATE AND FORTUNE

Dreadful is the mysterious power of fate—there is no deliverance from it by wealth or by war, by towered city, or dark, sea-beaten ships.

> **—Sophocles,** *Antigone*

But if you know that you are a man too, and that even such are those that rule, learn this first of all: that all human affairs are a wheel which, as it turns, does not allow the same men always to be fortunate.

> **—Herodotus,** *Histories*

The anvil of justice is planted firm,
and fate who makes the sword does the forging in advance.

> **—Aeschylus,** *The Libation Bearers*

The lot of man,—to suffer and to die.

 —Homer, *The Odyssey*

While our eyes wait to see the final destined day, we must call no mortal happy until he has crossed life's border free from pain.

 —Sophocles, *Oedipus Tyrannus*

The nobly born must nobly meet his fate.

 —Euripides, *Alcmene*

Circumstances rule men and not men circumstances.

 —Herodotus, *Histories*

Fortunate men stand in a certain relation to the divinity and love the gods, having confidence in them, owing to the benefits they have received from fortune.

 —Aristotle, *Rhetoric*

FRIENDSHIP

What is a friend? A single soul dwelling in two bodies.

 —Aristotle

Make no man your friend before inquiring how he has used his former friends; for you must expect him to treat you as he has treated them. Be slow to give your friendship, but when you have given it, strive to make it lasting; for it is as reprehensible to make many changes in one's associates as to have no friend at all. Neither test your friends to your own injury nor be willing to forgo a test of your companions. You can manage this if you pretend to be in want when really you lack nothing.

—Isocrates, letter to Demonicus

Sharing is a token of friendship; one does not want to share even a journey with one's enemies.

—Aristotle, *Politics*

You will best serve your friends if you do not wait for them to ask your help, but go of your own accord at the crucial moment to lend them aid.

—Isocrates, letter to Demonicus

It is the law of fate that evil can never be a friend to evil and that good must always be friend to good.

—Socrates, as quoted in Plato's *Phaedrus*

The wish for friendship develops rapidly, but friendship does not.

—Aristotle, *Ethics*

Regard as your most faithful friends, not those who praise everything you say or do, but those who criticize your mistakes.

—Isocrates, speech to Nicocles

Friendship exists only between good men, whereas the bad man never achieves true friendship with either a good or a bad man.

—Socrates, as quoted in Plato's *Lysis*

Goodwill seems therefore to be the beginning of friendship, just as the pleasure of the eye is the beginning of love.

—Aristotle, *Nicomachean Ethics*

If a man's companion [is] dirty, the person who keeps close company with him must of necessity get a share of his dirt, even though he himself happens to be clean.

—Epictetus, *Enchiridion*

Friendship is equality.

—Aristotle, *Ethics*

The base honor their friends only when they are present; the good cherish theirs even when they are far away; and while it takes only a short time to break up the intimacies of the base, not all eternity can blot out the friendships of good men.

—Isocrates, letter to Demonicus

Between friends there is no need for justice, but people who are just still need the quality of friendship; and indeed friendliness is considered to be justice in the fullest sense.

—**Aristotle,** *Ethics*

Choose for thy friend, the friend of virtue; yield to his gentle counsels, profit by his life, and for a trifling grievance never leave him.

—**Pythagoras**

It is characteristic of good men neither to go wrong themselves nor to allow their friends to do so.

—**Aristotle,** *Ethics*

All things are in common among friends.

—**Diogenes of Sinope, fragment**

GOSSIP

An evil tongue is sharper than the sharpest sword edge.

—**Strabo, fragment**

A wound by a sword is easier to bear than a wound by gossip.

—**Pythagoras, fragment**

Lay down for yourself, at the outset, a certain stamp and type of character for yourself, which you are to maintain whether you are by yourself or are meeting with people. And be silent for the most part, or else make only the most necessary remarks, and express these in few words. But rarely, and when occasion requires you to talk, talk, indeed, but about no ordinary topics. Do not talk about gladiators, or horseraces, or athletes, or things to eat or drink—topics that arise on all occasions; but above all, do not talk about people, either blaming, or praising, or comparing them.

—**Epictetus,** *Enchiridion*

HAPPINESS

It is virtuous activities that determine our happiness, and the opposite kind that produce the opposite effect.

—**Aristotle,** *Ethics*

Let no man be called happy before his death. Till then, he is not happy, only lucky.

—**Solon, fragment**

The joy that comes past hope and beyond expectation is like no other pleasure in extent.

—**Sophocles,** *Antigone*

One swallow does not make a summer; neither does one day. Similarly neither can one day, or a brief space of time, make a man blessed and happy.

—**Aristotle**, *Ethics*

Not knowing anything is the sweetest life.

—**Sophocles**, *Ajax*

Happiness demands not only complete goodness but a complete life.

—**Aristotle**, *Ethics*

HATE

Anger is always concerned with individuals, . . . whereas hatred is directed also against classes: We all hate any thief and any informer. Moreover, anger can be cured by time; but hatred cannot. The one aims at giving pain to its object, the other at doing him harm; the angry man wants his victim to feel; the hater does not mind whether they feel or not.

—**Aristotle**, *Rhetoric*

HUMANS AND HUMANITY

Man is the measure of all things.

—Protagoras, fragment

A lifetime is a child playing, playing checkers; the kingdom belongs to a child.

—Heraclitus, Fragments

You are a citizen of the world, and a part of it, not one of the parts destined for service, but one of primary importance; for you possess the faculty of understanding the divine administration of the world, and of reasoning upon the consequences thereof.

—Epictetus, *Discourses*

There are many wonderful things, but none is more wonderful than man.

—Sophocles, *Antigone*

A virtuous human being is the best of all animals, but one who has distanced himself from law and justice is the worst of all.

—Aristotle

Let mortal man keep to his own
mortality, and not expect too much.

—Euripides, *Alcestis*

If we are willing to survey human nature as a whole, we shall find that the majority of men do not take pleasure in the food that is the most wholesome, nor in the pursuits that are the most honorable, nor in the actions that are the noblest, nor in the creatures that are the most useful, but that they have tastes which are in every way contrary to their best interests, while they view those who have some regard for their duty as men of austere and laborious lives.

—Isocrates, letter to Nicocles

Different men sell themselves at different prices.

—Epictetus, *Discourses*

What is a man? A part of a state; first of that state which is made up of gods and men, and then of that which is said to be very close to the other, the state that is a small copy of the universal state.

—Epictetus, *Discourses*

To labor is the lot of man below;
And when Jove gave us life, he gave us woe.

—Homer, *The Iliad*

When we act pugnaciously, and injuriously, and angrily, and rudely, to what level have we degenerated? To the level of the wild beasts. Well, the fact is that some of us are wild beasts of a larger size, while others are little animals, malignant and petty.

—Epictetus, *Discourses*

There are many dreadful things but nothing is more dreadful than human beings.

> —Sophocles

A dreamlike feebleness by which the blind race of man is hampered.

> —Aeschylus, *Prometheus Bound*

There are not many very good or very bad people, but the great majority are something between the two.

> —Socrates, as quoted in **Plato's** *Phaedo*

A human being is only breath and shadow.

> —Sophocles, *Ajax*

HUMOR AND COMEDY

If you like me and the material I think up,
posterity will consider you to have had good taste!

> —Aristophanes

The buffoon is one who cannot resist a joke; he will not keep his tongue off himself or anyone else, if he can raise a laugh, and will say things which a man of refinement would never say, and some of which he would not even allow to be said to him.

—**Aristotle**, *Nicomachean Ethics*

It is the compelling power of great thoughts and ideas to engender phrases of equal size.

—**Aristophanes**, The *Frogs*

There's never been a happy man
who doesn't have a peaceful married life.

—**Aristophanes**, *Lysistrata*

No, I have no passion for battles; what I love is to drink with good comrades in the corner by the fire when good dry wood, cut in the height of the summer, is crackling; it is to cook peas on the coals and beechnuts among the embers; it is to kiss our pretty Thracian while my wife is at the bath.

—**Aristophanes**, *Peace*

IGNORANCE AND PETTINESS

It belongs to small-mindedness to be unable to bear either honor or dishonor, either good fortune or bad, but to be filled with conceit when honored and puffed up by trifling good fortune, and to be unable to bear even the smallest dishonor and to deem any chance failure a great misfortune, and to be distressed and annoyed at everything. Moreover the small-minded man is the sort of person to call all slights an insult and dishonor, even those that are due to ignorance or forgetfulness. Small-mindedness is accompanied by pettiness, querulousness, pessimism and self-abasement.

—**Aristotle,** *Virtues and Vices*

Hide our ignorance as we will, an evening of wine soon reveals it.

—**Heraclitus, fragment**

The poets were not alone in sanctioning myths, for long before the poets the states and the lawmakers had sanctioned them as a useful expedient. . . . They needed to control the people by superstitious fears, and these cannot be aroused without myths and marvels.

—**Strabo,** *Geographia*

They named it Ovation from the Latin *ovis* [a sheep].

—**Plutarch,** *Lives*

Keep closed thine eye and ear 'gainst prejudice.

—**Pythagoras**

Ignorance is a tough evil to conquer.

—**Sophocles**

Foolishness is indeed the sister of wickedness.

—**Sophocles, fragment**

INTELLIGENCE

As to reasoning, you are not inferior to the gods, nor less than they. For the greatness of reason is not determined by length nor by height, but by the decisions of its will.

—**Epictetus,** *Discourses*

No great genius has ever existed without some touch of madness.

—**Aristotle, fragment**

What, then, is the true nature of God? Flesh? Far from it! Land? Far from it! Fame? Far from it! It is intelligence, knowledge, right reason.

—**Epictetus,** *Discourses*

LOVE AND PASSION

One word frees us of all the weight and pain of life: "Love."
> —Sophocles, *Oedipus at Colonus*

Your lover is he who loves your soul.
> —Socrates, *Alcibiades*

When desire, having rejected reason and overpowered judgment which leads to right, is set in the direction of the pleasure which beauty can inspire, and when again under the influence of its kindred desires it is moved with violent motion towards the beauty of corporeal forms, it acquires a surname from this very violent motion, and is called "love."
> —Socrates, as quoted in Plato's *Phaedrus*

It's only the women of ripe age who understand the art of love.
> —Aristophanes, *The Ecclesiazusae*

Those who love each other on the ground of utility do not love each other for their personal qualities, but only in so far as they derive some benefit from each other. Similarly with those who love one another on the ground of pleasure.
> —Aristotle, *Ethics*

If a man is in love he is more daring than cowardly, and endures many dangers.
> —Aristotle, *Eudemian Ethics*

The young are prone to fall in love, as love is chiefly guided by emotion, and grounded on pleasure; hence they form attachments quickly and give them up quickly, often changing before the day is out.

—**Aristotle,** *Nicomachean Ethics*

Each man has his own particular weakness; as for me I am aflame with love for this virgin.

—**Aristophanes,** *The Thesmophoriazusae*

By "wicked" we mean that popular lover, who craves the body rather than the soul.

—**Plato,** *Symposium*

If lovers ought to be highly esteemed because they say they have the greatest love for the objects of their passion, since both by word and deed they are ready to make themselves hated by others to please the beloved, it is easy to see that, if what they say is true, whenever they fall in love afterwards, they will care for the new love more than for the old and will certainly injure the old love, if that pleases the new.

—**Plato,** *Phaedrus*

I may not know much else, I may be useless at other things, but somehow God's given me the power to recognize in an instant a man in love.

—**Socrates, as quoted in Plato's** *Lysis*

Love is the cause of unity in all things.

 —**Aristotle,** *Metaphysics*

I have seen people in tears of sorrow because of love and in slavery to the objects of their love, even though they believed before they fell in love that slavery is a great evil; I have seen them give those objects of their love many things that they could ill afford to part with; and I have seen people praying to be delivered from love just as from any other disease, and, for all that, unable to be delivered from it, but fettered by a stronger necessity than if they had been fettered with shackles of iron.

 —**Xenophon,** *Cyropaedia*

No oath is too binding for a lover.

 —**Sophocles,** *Phaedra*

We are the offspring of Eros; there are a thousand proofs to show it.

 —**Aristophanes,** *The Birds*

The fondness of the lover is not a matter of goodwill, but of appetite which he wishes to satisfy: Just as the wolf loves the lamb, so the lover adores his beloved.

 —**Socrates, as quoted in Plato's** *Phaedrus*

One can be loved without knowing it, but one cannot love without knowing it.

 —**Aristotle,** *Eudemian Ethics*

There is no sort of valor more respected by the gods than this which comes of love.

— Plato, *Symposium*

No one falls in love without first being charmed by beauty, but one may delight in another's beauty without necessarily being in love: One is in love only if one longs for the beloved when absent, and eagerly desires his presence.

— Aristotle, *Nicomachean Ethics*

He is no lover who does not love always.

— Aristotle, *Rhetoric*

Marry a good man and bear good children.

— King Leonidas of Sparta's last words to his wife, Gorgo, before departing with his army of three hundred to stop the Persians at Thermopylae, as quoted in Plutarch's *Sayings of Spartans*

Pleasures are a hindrance to thinking, and the more enjoyable they are, the greater the hindrance—for example, the pleasure of sex; for nobody could do anything against that background.

— Aristotle, *Ethics*

To love is to feel pleasure but to be loved is not; for being loved is not an activity of the thing loved, whereas loving is an activity— the activity of friendship; and loving occurs only in an animate thing, whereas being loved occurs with an inanimate thing also, for even inanimate things are loved.

—**Aristotle,** *Eudemian Ethics*

Love always begins in this manner: When men are happy not only in the presence of the beloved, but also in his absence when they recall him to mind.

—**Aristotle,** *Rhetoric*

MEN AND WOMEN

Of all things upon earth that bleed and grow,
A herb most bruised is woman.

—**Euripides,** *Medea*

Is there anyone to whom you commit more affairs of importance than you commit to your wife?

—**Socrates,** *Economics*

Woman is adept at getting money for herself and will not easily let herself be deceived; she understands deceit too well herself.

—**Aristophanes,** *The Ecclesiazusae*

Woman is woman's natural ally.

—**Euripides, fragment**

Tragic poets have a saying:
nothing's wilder than a woman!

—**Aristophanes,** *Lysistrata*

Man's best possession is a sympathetic wife.

—**Euripides,** *Antigone*

The oaths of a woman I inscribe on water.

—**Sophocles**

Silence is an ornament for women.

—**Sophocles,** *Ajax*

Mortals ought, you know, to beget children from some other source, and
there should be no female sex. Then mankind would have no trouble.

—**Euripides,** *Medea*

NECESSITY

There's no educator better than necessity.

—**Xenophon**

Never trust the advice of a man in difficulties.
  —Aesop

You cannot reason with a hungry belly; it has no ears.
  —Greek proverb

The might of Necessity permits no resistance.
  —Aeschylus, *Prometheus Bound*

I have soared aloft with poetry and with high thought, and though
I have laid my hand to many a reflection, I have found nothing
stronger than Necessity.
  —Euripides, *Alcestis*

Hunger is insolent, and will be fed.
  —Homer, *The Odyssey*

Not even Ares battles against necessity.
  —Sophocles

But I must bear my destiny as best I can,
knowing well that there is no resisting the strength of necessity.
  —Aeschylus, *Prometheus Bound*

NEGLECT

A man who is acting without thinking resembles a city with decrepit walls.

> **—Plato**

Carelessness brings many evils to man.

> **—Sophocles**

Those who, without thinking, waste good advice, soon are driven to evil acts.

> **—Menander, fragment**

PAIN AND SORROW

If you want to live your whole life free from pain you must become either a god or else a corpse. Consider other men's troubles and that will comfort you.

> **—Menander, fragment**

How sweet for those faring badly to forget their misfortunes even for a short time.

> **—Sophocles, fragment**

The origin of sorrow is this: to wish for something that does not come to pass.

—Epictetus, *Discourses*

To live without evil belongs only to the gods.

—Sophocles, fragment

Waste not fresh tears over old griefs.

—Euripides, fragment

There is some pleasure even in words, when they bring forgetfulness of present miseries.

—Sophocles, fragment

PARENTS AND CHILDREN

Conduct yourself toward your parents as you would have your children conduct themselves toward you.

—Isocrates, letter to Demonicus

He who is neglectful toward his parents is hated not only by humanity but also by the gods.

—Demosthenes, fragment

To give birth is a fearsome thing; there is no hating the child one has borne even when injured by it.

—**Sophocles,** *Electra*

Don't quarrel with your parents even if you are on the right.

—**Plato**

When parents die, the most modest funeral rites are the best, whereby the son neither exceeds the accustomed pomp, nor falls short of what his forefathers paid to their sires; and in like manner he should duly bestow the yearly attentions, which ensure honor, on the rites already completed.

—**Plato,** *Laws*

But whoever gives birth to useless children, what would you say of him except that he has bred sorrows for himself, and furnishes laughter for his enemies.

—**Sophocles,** *Antigone*

It's parents' blessings that support a home's foundations.

—**Plato**

Children are the anchors that hold a mother to life.

—**Sophocles, as quoted in Plato's** *Phaedra*

Children must respect their parents at home, respect strangers in the streets, and respect themselves when they are all alone.

—Demetrius of Phaleron

PUNISHMENT

Whom the gods wish to destroy, they first make mad.

—Euripides, *Antigone*

It is the nature of the many to be ruled by fear rather than by shame, and to refrain from evil not because of the disgrace but because of the punishments.

—Aristotle, *Ethics*

Slowly but surely withal moveth the might of the gods.

—Euripides, *Bacchae*

Knavery is the best defense against a knave.

—Zeno of Citium, as quoted in Plutarch's *Of Bashfulness*

The gods visit the sins of the fathers upon the children.

—Euripides, fragment

This just penalty ought to come straightaway upon all who would break the laws: the penalty of death. Then wrongdoing would not abound.

—**Sophocles,** *Electra*

RELATIONSHIPS

An unapparent connection is stronger than an apparent one.

—**Heraclitus, fragment**

Familiarity breeds contempt.

—**Aesop,** *Fables*

Listen to what men say about each other and try to discern at the same time the character of those who speak and of those about whom they speak.

—**Isocrates, speech to Nicocles**

SLEEP AND REST

Too much rest becomes a pain.

—**Homer,** *The Odyssey*

Much sleep is not required by nature, either for our souls or bodies, or for the actions in which they are concerned.

—**Plato,** *Protagoras*

While they are awake, all men are in one common world, but when asleep, each is in a world of his own.

—**Plutarch,** *Morals*

REVENGE

To take vengeance on one's enemies is nobler than to come to terms with them; for to retaliate is just, and that which is just is noble; and further, a courageous man ought not to allow himself to be beaten.

—**Aristotle,** *Rhetoric*

Men regard it as their right to return evil for evil and if they cannot, feel they have lost their liberty.

—**Aristotle,** *Nicomachean Ethics*

All of a man's affairs become diseased when he wishes to cure evils by evils.

—**Sophocles, fragment**

Bitter people are hard to reconcile, and keep up their anger for a long time, because they suppress their animosity. Relief comes only with retaliation; for revenge provides release from anger by substituting pleasure for pain. In default of this they still labor under the weight of resentment; because owing to its concealment nobody helps to persuade the sufferer out of it, and it takes him time to digest his anger internally. People of this kind cause a great deal of trouble to themselves and their closest friends.

—**Aristotle,** *Ethics*

Isn't it the sweetest mockery to mock our enemies?

—**Sophocles,** *Ajax*

Gentleness [is the] ability to bear reproaches and slights with moderation, and not to embark on revenge quickly, and not to be easily provoked to anger, but [be] free from bitterness and contentiousness, having tranquillity and stability in the spirit.

—**Aristotle,** *Virtues and Vices*

RUSHING

Don't rush. There is a perfect moment for everything we do.

—**Theognis, fragment**

Second thoughts are ever wiser.
>—**Euripides, fragment**

How prone to doubt, how cautious are the wise!
>—**Homer,** *The Odyssey*

Men should pledge themselves to nothing; for reflection makes a liar of their resolution.
>—**Sophocles,** *Antigone*

SECRETS

Guard more faithfully the secret which is confided to you than the money which is entrusted to your care; for good men ought to show that they hold their honor more trustworthy than an oath. Consider that you owe it to yourself no less to mistrust bad men than to put your trust in the good. On matters which you would keep secret, speak to no one save when it is equally expedient for you who speak and for those who hear that the facts should not be published.
>—**Isocrates, letter to Demonicus**

Everything is plainer when spoken than when unspoken.
>—**Socrates, as quoted in Plato's** *Phaedrus*

Confide in [your friends] about matters which require no secrecy as if they were secrets; for if you fail you will not injure yourself, and if you succeed you will have a better knowledge of their character.

—Isocrates, letter to Demonicus

SELF-DECEPTION

Nothing is easier than self-deceit because what each man wishes, he also believes to be true.

—Demosthenes, *Third Olynthiac*

The fly sat upon the axel-tree of the chariot wheel and said, "What a dust do I raise!"

—Aesop, *Fables*

If any man thinks that he alone is wise—that in speech or in mind he has no peer—such a soul, when laid open, is always found empty.

—Sophocles, *Antigone*

A time will soon come when the tragic actors will think that their masks and buskins and the long robes are . . . themselves.

—Epictetus, *Discourses*

Beware that you do not lose the substance by grasping at the shadow.

    —**Aesop,** *Fables*

Hope is the dream of a waking man.

    —**Aristotle, attributed to by Diogenes Laërtius in** *Lives of Eminent Philosophers*

To many men much-wandering hope comes as a boon, but to many others it is the deception of vain desires.

    —**Sophocles,** *Antigone*

If someone were to put a proposition before men bidding them choose, after examination, the best customs in the world, each nation would certainly select its own.

    —**Herodotus,** *Histories*

SELF-DESTRUCTION

Every enterprise of the thoughtless man is in vain.

    —**Menander, fragment**

Thoughtlessness is a bad function of the mind; a cause of base life.

    —**Aristotle, fragment**

Thoughtlessness is a self-imposed evil.

    —Hesiod, fragment

The thoughtless man is conquered by his desires.

    —Menander, fragment

Folly [is having] bad judgment of affairs, bad counsel, bad fellow-ship, bad use of one's resources, false opinions about what is fine and good in life. Folly is accompanied by unskillfulness, ignorance, uncontrol, awkwardness, forgetfulness.

    —Aristotle, *Virtues and Vices*

Time [is] the most valuable thing that a man could waste.

    —Theophrastus, fragment

Of ill-temper there are three kinds: Irascibility, bitterness, sullen-ness. It belongs to the ill-tempered man to be unable to bear either small slights or defeats but to be given to retaliation and revenge, and easily moved to anger by any chance deed or word. Ill-temper is accompanied by excitability of character, instability, bitter speech, and liability to take offence at trifles and to feel these feelings quickly and on slight occasions.

    —Aristotle, *Virtues and Vices*

To seek death in order to escape from poverty, or the pangs of love, or from pain or sorrow, is not the act of a courageous man, but rather of a coward; for it is weakness to fly from troubles, and the suicide does not endure death because it is noble to do so, but to escape evil.

—**Aristotle,** *Nicomachean Ethics*

Perverse Temptation, the overmastering child of designing Destruction, drives men on; and every remedy is futile.

—**Aeschylus,** *Agamemnon*

Those who are base in judgment do not know the good they hold in their hands until they cast it off.

—**Sophocles,** *Ajax*

Bestow your favors on the good; for a goodly treasury is a store of gratitude laid up in the heart of an honest man. If you benefit bad men, you will have the same reward as those who feed stray dogs; for these snarl alike at those who give them food and at the passing stranger; and just so base men wrong alike those who help and those who harm them.

—**Isocrates, letter to Demonicus**

SELF-INTEREST

Even wisdom has to yield to self-interest.

—**Pindar,** *Pythian Odes*

Bad people take no pleasure in each other unless there is a chance of some benefit.

>—**Aristotle,** *Ethics*

The injuries we cause and those we suffer are seldom weighed in the same scale.

>—**Aesop,** *Fables*

It is a general rule . . . that every living thing is to nothing so devoted as to its own interest.

>—**Epictetus,** *Discourses*

The first inclination which an animal has is to protect itself.

>—**Zeno of Citium, fragment**

It is best for the wise man not to seem wise.

>—**Aeschylus,** *Prometheus Bound*

Everyone is bound to bear patiently the results of his own example.

>—**Phaedrus,** *Fables*

SELF-RELIANCE

The gods help those that help themselves.

    —**Aesop,** *Fables*

Heaven never helps the man who will not act.

    —**Socrates, fragment**

God always strives together with those who strive.

    —**Aeschylus, fragment**

A word does not frighten the man who, in acting, feels no fear.

    —**Sophocles,** *Oedipus in Colonus*

You may always be victorious if you will never enter into any contest where the issue does not wholly depend upon yourself.

    —**Epictetus,** *Enchiridion*

Great things are won by great dangers.

    —**Herodotus,** *Histories*

Sickness is a hindrance to the body, but not to your ability to choose, unless that is your choice. Lameness is a hindrance to the leg, but not to your ability to choose. Say this to yourself with regard to everything that happens, then you will see such obstacles as hindrances to something else, but not to yourself.

    —**Epictetus,** *Enchiridion*

Fortune cannot aid those who do nothing.
—**Sophocles,** *Minos*

Try first thyself, and after call in God;
For to the worker God himself lends aid.
—**Euripides, fragment**

Whenever a man makes haste, God too hastens with him.
—**Aeschylus,** *The Persians*

SELF-SUFFICIENCY

The self-sufficient man is the richest among humans.
—**Menander, fragment**

Guard carefully what you possess but always seek the best.
—**Isocrates, fragment**

Self-sufficiency is both a good and an absolute good.
—**Aristotle,** *Politics*

You must have just enough property so that no one threatens you
nor are you missing life's necessities.
—**Plato**

He who is not aware of his own strength neglects his own self.

—Xenophon, fragment

SUCCESS

Success is man's god.

—**Aeschylus,** *Choephorae*

Remember, nothing succeeds without toil.

—**Sophocles,** *Electra*

Along with success comes a reputation for wisdom.

—**Euripides,** *Hippolytus*

From a small seed a mighty trunk may grow.

—**Aeschylus,** *The Libation Bearers*

SUPERSTITION

With [humanity] a word is an omen, you call a sneeze an omen, a meeting an omen, an unknown sound an omen, a slave or an ass an omen.

>—**Aristophanes**, *The Birds*

One omen is best, to fight for one's country.

>—**Homer**, *The Iliad*

TRANSIENCE

Life is short, art long, opportunity fleeting, experience treacherous, judgment difficult.

>—**Hippocrates**, *Aphorisms*

Today is today. Tomorrow we may be ourselves gone down the drain of eternity.

>—**Euripides**, *Alcestis*

A generation of mankind is like a generation of leaves. The wind scatters the leaves on the ground, but the living tree blossoms with leaves again in the spring.

>—**Homer**, *The Iliad*

But what says Zeus? "Epictetus, had it been possible I should have made both this paltry body and this small estate of thine free and unhampered. But as it is—let it not escape thee—this body is not thine own, but only clay cunningly compounded."

—Epictetus, *Discourses*

I see the state of all of us who live, nothing more than phantoms or a weightless shadow.

—Sophocles, *Ajax*

All is flux, nothing ever stays still.

—Heraclitus, fragment

The shimmering night does not stay for mortals, not misfortunes, nor wealth, but in a moment it is gone, and to the turn of another comes joy and loss.

—Sophocles, *The Women of Trachis*

Consider that nothing in human life is stable; for then you will not exult overmuch in prosperity, nor grieve overmuch in adversity. Rejoice over the good things which come to you, but grieve in moderation over the evils which befall you.

—Isocrates, letter to Isocrates

History is a child building a sand-castle by the sea, and that child is the whole majesty of man's power in the world.

—Heraclitus, fragment

Alas, generations of mortals, how mere a shadow I count your life!

> —**Sophocles,** *Oedipus Tyrannus*

Time is the image of eternity.

> —**Plato, as quoted by Diogenes Laërtius in** *Lives of Eminent Philosophers*

VEGETARIANISM

. . . Not only to abstain from [eating] living things, but also never to approach butchers and huntsmen.

> —**Pythagoras' maxims, from Porphyrius'** *Vita Pythagorae*

WAR AND PEACE

Wars and revolutions and battles are due simply and solely to the body and its desires. All wars are undertaken for the acquisition of wealth; and the reason why we have to acquire wealth is the body, because we are slaves in its service.

> —**Socrates, as quoted in Plato's** *Phaedo*

It is not the object of war to annihilate those who have given provocation for it, but to cause them to mend their ways; not to ruin the innocent and guilty alike, but to save both.

—Polybius, *Histories*

In peace sons bury fathers. War violates the order of nature and fathers bury sons.

—Herodotus, *Histories*

War is the last of all things to go according to schedule.

—Thucydides, *The History of the Peloponnesian War*

I should like to know how we are to give advice to the Athenians as to making war or not, if we do not know in what their strength consists, whether it is naval, military, or both, how great it is, their sources of revenue, their friends and enemies, and further, what wars they have already waged, with what success, and all similar things?

—Aristotle, *Rhetoric*

Peace with justice and honor is the fairest and most profitable of possessions, but with disgrace and cowardice it is the most infamous and harmful of all.

—Polybius, *Histories*

Victory shifteth from man to man.

—Homer, *The Iliad*

The execution of a military surprise is always dangerous and the general who is never taken off his guard himself, and never loses an opportunity of striking at an unguarded foe, will be most likely to succeed in war.

—Thucydides, *The History of the Peloponnesian War*

Another such victory over the Romans, and we are finished.

—Pyrrhus, as quoted in Plutarch's *Lives*

Victory is pleasant, not only to those who love to conquer, but to all; for there is produced an idea of superiority, which all with more or less eagerness desire.

—Aristotle, *Rhetoric*

'T is man's to fight, but Heaven's to give success.

—Homer, *The Iliad*

Our business in the field of fight
Is not to question, but to prove our might.

—Homer, *The Iliad*

War never takes a wicked man by chance, the good man always.

—Sophocles, *Philoctetes*

It is necessary to know that war is common and right is strife and that all things happen by strife and necessity.

—Heraclitus, fragment

You can be invincible if you never enter a contest in which victory is not under your control.

      —**Epictetus**, *Enchiridion*

We make war that we may live in peace.

      —**Aristotle**, *Ethics*

In a just cause the weak o'ercome the strong.

      —**Sophocles**, *Oedipus at Colonus*

War loves to seek its victims in the young.

      —**Sophocles**, *Scyrii*

The objects at stake in a war against the barbarian are nothing less than our country, our life, our habits, our freedom, and all such blessings.

      —**Demosthenes**, *Speeches*

WEALTH AND POVERTY

There are some who praise a man free from disease; to me no man who is poor seems free from disease but to be constantly sick.

      —**Sophocles, fragment**

Excessive riches mean no advantage for mortals, and when a god is angry at a house, they make the ruin greater.

—Euripides, *Medea*

Silver and gold will not make men better. It is the opinions of wise men that enrich with virtue those who share them.

—Plato

Wealth does not bring goodness, but goodness brings wealth and every other blessing, both to the individual and to the state.

—Socrates, as quoted in Plato's *Apology*

Silver and gold are not the only coin; virtue too passes current all over the world.

—Euripides, fragment

When a man craves to acquire wealth ignobly, or feels no qualm in so acquiring it, he does not then by his gifts pay honor to his soul—far from it, in sooth!

—Plato, *Laws*

He who spends rightly acquired fortune in good deeds may never become exceedingly rich but also, he will never be a poor man.

—Plato

Everybody loves a thing more if it has cost him trouble: for instance those who have made money love money more than those who have inherited it.

—**Aristotle,** *Nicomachean Ethics*

Money is to be kept at a distance if one doesn't know how to use it.

—**Socrates,** *Economics*

Money is the worst currency that ever grew among mankind. This sacks cities, this drives men from their homes, this teaches and corrupts the worthiest minds to turn base deeds.

—**Sophocles,** *Antigone*

No one goes to Hades with all his immense wealth.

—**Theognis,** *Maxims*

Those whose life is long still strive for gain, and for all mortals all things take second place to money.

—**Sophocles, fragment**

False shame accompanies a man that is poor, shame that either harms a man greatly or profits him; shame is with poverty, but confidence with wealth.

—**Hesiod,** *Works and Days*

The company of just and righteous men is better than wealth and a rich estate.

—**Euripides, fragment**

Of prosperity mortals can never have enough.

—**Aeschylus,** *Agamemnon*

A prosperous fool is a grievous burden.

—**Aeschylus, fragment**

EDUCATION AND LEARNING

EDUCATION

He who seeks knowledge must desire, from a young age, to hear the entire truth.

—**Plato,** *The Republic*

The beginning of every government starts with the education of our youth.

—**Pythagoras**

We ought to esteem it of the greatest importance that the stories which children first hear should be adapted in the most perfect manner to the promotion of virtue.

—**Socrates, as quoted in Plato's** *The Republic*

Even noble souls can become corrupted with wrong education.

    —Plato, *The Republic*

The soul tends to cower before a moral lesson rather than before a physical exercise because physical exercises it shares with the body but moral lessons it bears by itself.

    —Plato, *The Republic*

After the age of six, each sex shall be kept separate, boys spending their time with boys, and likewise girls with girls; and when it is necessary for them to begin lessons, the boys must go to teachers of riding, archery, javelin-throwing and slinging; and the girls also, if they agree to it, must share in the lessons, and especially such as relate to the use of arms.

    —Plato, *Laws*

To become self-educated you should condemn yourself for all those things that you would criticize others.

    —Diogenes of Sinope

Youth should stay away from all evil, especially things that produce wickedness and ill-will.

    —Aristotle, *Politics*

If we don't mold clay, it does not become a ceramic.

    —Xenophon

Our youth should also be educated with music and physical education.

     —Aristotle, *Politics*

Physical work, even if it is done by the body against its will, will not harm the body. Lessons, however, that enter the soul against its will never grow roots and will never be preserved inside it.

     —Plato, *The Republic*

The roots of education are bitter, but the fruit is sweet.

     —Aristotle

From all wild beasts, a child is the most difficult to handle.

     —Plato

Only the educated are free.

     —Epictetus, *Discourses*

Why not whip the teacher when the pupil misbehaves?

     —Diogenes of Sinope, fragment

I swear . . . to hold my teacher in this art equal to my own parents; to make him partner in my livelihood; when he is in need of money to share mine with him; to consider his family as my own brothers and to teach them this art, if they want to learn it, without fee or indenture.

     —Hippocrates, Hippocratic Oath

It is a mark of much folly not to have one's life regulated with regard to some End.

—**Aristotle,** *Eudemian Ethics*

All skill and education aim at filling the gaps that nature leaves.

—**Aristotle,** *Politics*

[Regarding education,] to be constantly asking "What is the use of it?" is unbecoming to those of broad vision and unworthy of free men.

—**Aristotle,** *Politics*

What is a child? Ignorance. What is a child? Want of instruction.

—**Epictetus,** *Discourses*

Thoughts are mightier than strength of hand.

—**Sophocles,** *Phaedra*

If my body is enslaved, still my mind is free.

—**Sophocles**

We must remember that one man is much the same as another, and that he is best who is trained in the severest school.

—**Thucydides,** *The History of the Peloponnesian War*

EXPERIENCE

Anything that we have to learn to do we learn by the actual doing of it: People become builders by building and instrumentalists by playing instruments. Similarly we become just by performing just acts, temperate by performing temperate ones, brave by performing brave ones.

—**Aristotle,** *Ethics*

Consider that as the best thing which we have from the gods is good fortune, so the best thing which we have in ourselves is good judgment.

—**Isocrates, letter to Demonicus**

It is from memory that men acquire experience, because the numerous memories of the same thing eventually produce the effect of a single experience.

—**Aristotle,** *Metaphysics*

Nothing great comes into being all at once.

—**Epictetus,** *Discourses*

There are no experienced young people. Time makes experience.

—**Aristotle**

Let there be nothing untried; for nothing happens by itself, but men obtain all things by trying.

—**Herodotus,** *Histories*

Practice is everything.

> —**Periander, as quoted by Diogenes Laërtius in** *Lives of Eminent Philosophers*

The fool learns by suffering.

> —**Hesiod,** *Works and Days*

KNOWLEDGE

What is to be taught I learn; what is to be discovered I seek; what is to be prayed for I sought from the gods.

> —**Sophocles, fragment**

All men by nature desire knowledge.

> —**Aristotle,** *Metaphysics*

I grow old, ever learning many things.

> —**Solon**

We must take care of our minds because we cannot benefit from beauty when our brains are missing.

> —**Euripides, fragment**

Not by ignorance but by deep learning can people judge properly.

—Plato, *The Republic*

If you love knowledge, you will be a master of knowledge. What you have come to know, preserve by exercise; what you have not learned, seek to add to your knowledge; for it is as reprehensible to hear a profitable saying and not grasp it as to be offered a good gift by one's friends and not accept it.

—Isocrates, letter to Demonicus

Instruct thyself, for time and patience favor all.

—Pythagoras

The only real ill-doing is the deprivation of knowledge.

—Plato, *Protagoras*

Entire ignorance is not so terrible or extreme an evil, and is far from being the greatest of all; too much cleverness and too much learning, accompanied with ill bringing-up, are far more fatal.

—Plato, *Protagoras*

ARTS AND SCIENCES

ART

He who neglects the arts when young has lost the past and is dead
to the future.

    —Sophocles, fragment

All things desire and love existence; but we exist in activity, since we
exist by living and doing; and in a sense one who has made something exists actively, and so he loves his handiwork because he loves
existence.

    —Aristotle, *Nicomachean Ethics*

If the better is the less vulgar and the less vulgar is always that
which appeals to the better audience, then obviously the art which
makes its appeal to everybody is eminently vulgar.

    —Aristotle, *Poetics*

BIOLOGY

Man is a biped without feathers.

—**Plato,** *Politics*

BUSINESS AND MANAGEMENT

It will not always be summer; build barns.

—**Hesiod,** *Works and Days*

The way to make money is to get, if you can, a monopoly for yourself.

—**Aristotle,** *Politics*

Admire a small ship, but put your freight in a large one; for the larger the load, the greater will be the profit upon profit.

—**Hesiod,** *Works and Days*

The excessive increase of anything causes a reaction in the opposite direction.

—**Plato,** *The Republic*

When you put men in charge of affairs which are not under your personal direction, be governed by the knowledge that you your-self will be held responsible for whatever they do.

      —Isocrates, speech to Nicocles

Never look for your work in one place and your progress in another.

      —Epictetus, *Discourses*

If you add a little to a little, and then do it again, soon that little shall be much.

      —Hesiod, *Works and Days*

COSMOLOGY

The cosmos is the most beautiful thing of everything that exists.

      —Plato

. . . Of the infinite there is no beginning . . . but this [void] seems to be the beginning of the other things, and to surround all things and steer all, as all those say who do not postulate other causes, such as mind or love, above and beyond the infinite. And this is the divine; for it is immortal and indestructible.

      —Aristotle, *Physics*

By the original composition of the universe, sky and earth had one form, their natures being mingled; after this their bodies parted from each other, and the world took on the whole agreement that we see in it.

—Diodorus Siculus, fragment

[Anaximander] said that the principle and element of existing things was the infinite. . . . (In addition to this he said that motion was eternal, in which it results that the heavens come into being.) . . . He said that the material principle of existing things was some nature coming under the heading of the infinite, from which come into being the heavens and the world in them. This nature is eternal and unaging, and it also surrounds all the worlds.

—Anaximander, as quoted by Hippolytus

All the physicists make the infinite a property of some other nature belonging to the so-called elements, such as water or air or that which is intermediate between these.

—Aristotle, *Physics*

For [Anaximander] thought that things were born not from one substance, as Thales thought from water, but each from its own particular principles. These principles of individual things he believed to be infinite, and to give birth to innumerable worlds and whatsoever arises in them; and those worlds, he thought, are now dissolved, now born again, according to the age to which each is able to survive.

—Anaximander, as quoted by Cicero

The Earth is [suspended], held up by nothing, but remaining on account of its similar distance from all things.

  —Anaximander, as quoted by Hippolytus

The world, an entity out of everything, was created by neither gods nor men, but was, is, and will be eternally living fire, regularly becoming ignited and regularly becoming extinguished.

  —Heraclitus, fragment

Democritus holds the same view as Leucippus about the elements, full and void . . . he spoke as if the things that are were in constant motion in the void; and there are innumerable worlds, which differ in size. In some worlds there is no sun and moon, in others they are larger than in our world, and in others more numerous. The intervals between the worlds are unequal; in some parts there are more worlds, in others fewer; some are increasing, some at their height, some decreasing; in some parts they are arising, in others failing. They are destroyed by collision one with another. There are some worlds devoid of living creatures or plants or any moisture.

  —Democritus, as quoted by Hippolytus

Even sleepers are workers and collaborators on what goes on in the universe.

  —Heraclitus, fragment

Moreover, the universe as a whole is infinite, for whatever is limited has an outermost edge to limit it, and such an edge is defined by something beyond. Since the universe has no edge, it has no limit; and since it lacks a limit, it is infinite and unbounded. Moreover, the universe is infinite both in the number of its atoms and in the extent of its void.

—Epicurus, *Letters*

DISCOVERY

If one does not expect the unexpected, one will not find it out, since it is not to be searched out, and difficult to compass.

—**Heraclitus, as quoted in Clement's** *Stromateis*

And Archimedes, as he was washing, thought of a manner of computing the proportion of gold in King Hiero's crown by seeing the water flowing over the bathing-stool. He leaped up as one possessed or inspired, crying, "I have found it! Eureka!"

—**Plutarch**

EVOLUTION

Further, [Anaximander] says that in the beginning man was born from creatures of a different kind; because other creatures are soon self-supporting, but man alone needs prolonged nursing. For this reason he would not have survived if this had been his original form.

—**Plutarch,** *Stromateis Istorikoi*

For we all came forth from earth and water.

—**Xenophanes, as quoted in Sextus'** *Advanced Mathematics*

Nothing can be produced out of nothing.

—**Diogenes of Apollonia, fragment**

HEALTH

One should eat to live and not live to eat.

—**Socrates**

Alcmaeon maintains that the bond of health is the "equal balance" of the powers, moist and dry, cold and hot, bitter and sweet, and the rest, while the "supremacy" of one of them is the cause of disease; for the supremacy of either is destructive. Illness comes about directly through excess of heat or cold, indirectly through surfeit or deficiency of nourishment; and its center is either the blood or the marrow or the brain. It sometimes arises in these centers from external causes, moisture of some sort or environment or exhaustion or hardship or similar causes. Health on the other hand is the proportionate admixture of the qualities.

—Alcmaeon of Croton, as quoted by Aetius

Every eccentricity arises from some human trait, but [uncleanliness] comes close to being non-human.

—Epictetus, *Discourses*

Extreme remedies are very appropriate for extreme diseases.

—Hippocrates, *Aphorisms*

A wise doctor does not mutter incantations over a sore that needs the knife.

—Sophocles, *Ajax*

It is a sign of a dull nature to occupy oneself deeply in matters that concern the body; for instance, to be overly occupied about exercise, about eating and drinking, about easing oneself, about sexual intercourse.

—Epictetus, *Enchiridion*

Health is a thing you ought not to despise; in diet use a mean, and exercise; and that's a mean whence does no damage rise.

—Pythagoras

When we say that pleasure is the end, we do not mean the pleasure of the profligate or that which depends on physical enjoyment—as some think who do not understand our teachings, disagree with them, or give them an evil interpretation—but by pleasure we mean the state wherein the body is free from pain and the mind from anxiety.

—Epicurus, *Letters*

NATURE

The one teacher of virtue and freedom to all humanity is nature.

—Menander, fragment

Nature does not aim to deceive. Everything that it produces it does so with clarity and truth.

—Xenophon, *Estate Management*

We all know that as we are beneficent toward nature, it becomes beneficent toward us.

—Xenophon, *Estate Management*

Earth gives birth to everything and yet it continues to give.

—Menander, fragment

God and nature do nothing in vain.

—Aristotle, *Politics*

PHILOSOPHY

Philosophy begins in wonder.

—Plato, *Theaetetus*

What is the first business of one who practices philosophy? To get rid of thinking that one knows; for it is impossible to get a man to begin to learn that which he thinks he knows.

—Epictetus, *Discourses*

Philosophy, the love of wisdom, is impossible for the multitude.

—Plato, *The Republic*

Of what use is a philosopher who doesn't hurt anybody's feelings?

—Diogenes of Sinope, fragment

The epithet "wise" is too great and befits God alone; but the name "philosopher," that is, "lover of wisdom," or something of the sort would be more fitting and modest for a man.

—Socrates, as quoted in Plato's *Phaedrus*

Life . . . is like a festival; just as some come to the festival to compete, some to ply their trade, but the best people come as spectators, so in life the slavish men go hunting for fame or gain, the philosophers for the truth.

—Pythagoras, as quoted by Diogenes Laërtius in *Lives of Eminent Philosophers*

For it is owing to their wonder that men both now begin and at first began to philosophize. . . . And a man who is puzzled and wonders thinks himself ignorant; therefore since they philosophized in order to escape from ignorance, evidently they were pursuing science in order to know, and not for any utilitarian end.

—Aristotle, *Metaphysics*

With prudence the Philosopher approves or blames; If Errors triumph, he departs and waits.

—Pythagoras

PHYSICAL EDUCATION

When a body becomes soft, the soul also weakens.

—Socrates

Train your body, not by the exercises which conduce to strength, but by those which conduce to health. In this you will succeed if you cease your exertions while you still have energy to exert yourself.

—Isocrates, letter to Demonicus

Both excessive and deficient exercise ruins physical strength.

—Aristotle

Strive with your body to be a lover of toil, and with your soul to be a lover of wisdom, in order that with the one you may have the strength to carry out your resolves, and with the other the intelligence to foresee what is for your good.

—Isocrates, letter to Demonicus

POETRY

A poet . . . is a light thing, and winged and holy, and cannot compose before he gets inspiration.

—Socrates, as quoted in Plato's *Ion*

A poet's object is not to tell what actually happened but what could or would happen either probably or inevitably. . . . For this reason poetry is something more scientific and serious than history, because poetry tends to give general truths while history gives particular facts.

—Aristotle, *Poetics*

The poet should speak as seldom as possible in his own character, since he is not "representing" the story in that sense.

—Aristotle, *Poetics*

So I soon made up my mind about the poets too: I decided that it was not wisdom that enabled them to write their poetry, but a kind of instinct or inspiration, such as you find in seers and prophets who deliver all their sublime messages without knowing in the least what they mean.

—Socrates, as quoted in Plato's *Apology*

The more serious poets represented fine doings and the doings of fine men, while those of a less exalted nature represented the actions of inferior men, at first writing satire just as the others at first wrote hymns and eulogies.

—Aristotle, *Poetics*

The god relieves [poets] of their reason and uses them as his ministers, just as he uses soothsayers and divine prophets—so that we who listen to them may realize that it is not they who say such supremely valuable things as they do, who have not reason in them, but that it is the god himself who speaks, and addresses us through them.

—Socrates, as quoted in Plato's *Ion*

Epic poetry, then, and the poetry of tragic drama, and, moreover, comedy and dithyrambic poetry, and most flute-playing and harp-playing, these, speaking generally, may all be said to be "representations of life."

—Aristotle, *Poetics*

Painting [is] silent poetry, and poetry speaking painting.

—Simonides, as quoted by Plutarch

PUBLIC SPEAKING

The measure of a speech is not the orator but the listener.

—Plato

It's a terrible thing to speak well and be wrong.

—Sophocles, *Electra*

Much speech is one thing, well-timed speech is another.

—Sophocles, *Oedipus at Colonus*

SCIENCE AND METHODOLOGY

All opinions without scientific base are worthless.

—Plato, *The Republic*

To discover what is natural we must study it preferably in things that are in a natural state, and not in specimens that are degenerate.

—**Aristotle,** *Politics*

To be a successful farmer one must first know the nature of the soil.

—**Xenophon,** *Economics*

Science divorced from justice and virtue appears to be villainy and not wisdom.

—**Plato**

Proper knowledge is hard to obtain.

—**Pittacus, fragment**

Give me where to stand, and I will move the earth.

—**Archimedes, fragment**

SENSES

Nothing exists in thought that wasn't first perceived through your senses.

—**Plato**

For man ... differs from other animals in that he only understands, while the rest perceive but do not understand, thought and perception being different, not ... the same.

—Alcmaeon of Croton, as quoted in Theophrastus' *De Sensu*

By convention there is color, by convention sweetness, by convention bitterness, but in reality there are atoms and space.

—Democritus, fragment

For as the body grows old, so the wits grow old and become blind towards all things alike.

—Herodotus, *Histories*

SPECIALIZATION

All things will be produced in superior quantity and quality, and with greater ease, when each man works at a single occupation, in accordance with his natural gifts, and at the right moment, without meddling with anything else.

—Plato, *The Republic*

We should not take heed to what many say but what the specialist will say.

> —Plato, *The Republic*

Men who wish to know about the world must learn about it in its particular details.

> —Heraclitus, fragment

It is much better to learn one thing well than to know many things partially.

> —Menander

Hardly any human being is capable of pursuing two professions or two arts rightly.

> —Gorgias, fragment

THE STATE

DEMOCRACY

We call democracy the sum of its citizenry.
> —Thucydides

A democracy exists whenever those who are free and are not well-off, being in the majority, are in sovereign control of government.
> —Aristotle, *Politics*

There is one safeguard known generally to the wise, which is an advantage and security to all, but especially to democracies, against despots: Distrust.
> —Demosthenes, *Second Philippic*

Regarding political governing, not for it to be permanent [in the hands of the same people] this is democracy.

—Aristotle, *Politics*

Governments which have a regard to the common interest are constituted in accordance with strict principles of justice, and are therefore true forms; but those which regard only the interest of the rulers are all defective and perverted forms, for they are despotic, whereas a state is a community of freemen.

—Aristotle, *Politics*

Democratic governments are altered by the shamelessness of demagogues.

—Aristotle, *Politics*

In the best democratic state it's impossible for rogues to govern and virtuous men not to govern.

—Pittacus

[In oligarchies] the struggle to get rich at all costs tended to reduce numbers [of rich rulers] and so increased the power of the multitude, who rose up and formed democracies.

—Aristotle, *Politics*

Democracy is an agreeable, lawless, multicolored commonwealth, dealing with all alike on equal terms, whether they be really equal or not.

—**Plato,** *The Republic*

There are two marks by which democracy is thought to be defined: "sovereignty of the majority" and "liberty."

—**Aristotle,** *Politics*

Our constitution does not copy the laws of neighboring states; we are rather a pattern to others than imitators ourselves. Its administration favors the many instead of the few; this is why it is called a democracy.

—**Pericles, "Funeral Oration," as quoted in Thucydides'**
The History of the Peloponnesian War

Oligarchies and democracies seek equality for those who share in the administration of them; and the doctrine is in high favor in those governments that one man should not have the power to get more than another—a principle which works in the interest of the worthless!

—**Isocrates,** *The Cyprians*

Unlike any other nation, regarding him who takes no part in these duties not as unambitious but as useless, we Athenians are able to judge at all events if we cannot originate, and, instead of looking on discussion as a stumbling-block in the way of action, we think it an indispensable preliminary to any wise action at all.

—Pericles, "Funeral Oration," as quoted in Thucydides'
The History of the Peloponnesian War

GOVERNMENT AND POLITICS

Man is by nature a political animal.

—Aristotle, *Politics*

The punishment of wise men who refuse to take part in the government is to live under the government of worse men.

—Plato, *The Republic*

We should educate our youth regarding the governing of the state.

—Aristotle, *Politics*

The leader [of the city] must remember three things: first that he reigns over people, second that he reigns according to the laws, and third that he will not reign forever.

—Agathon, fragment

Take care of your citizens and try, most of all, to keep them happy knowing that of all political systems the ones that keep their citizens happy last the longest.

—Isocrates, letter to Demonicus

The leader is elected not to take care of himself, while in power, but to make sure those who elected him to rule over them are satisfied.

—Xenophon, *Memoirs*

If the leader is not wise and just, how can he rule properly?

—Aristotle, *Politics*

It's equally dangerous giving a madman a knife and a villain power.

—Socrates

Why do [Athenians] grow tired of being well served many times by the same men?

—Themistocles, *Sayings of Kings and Commanders*

You vote yourselves salaries out of the public funds and care only for your own personal interests; hence the state limps along.

—Aristophanes, *The Ecclesiazusae*

When a person of evil nature takes power, the public should be prepared for disasters.

—Aeschines, fragment

You must care for the people and make it your first consideration to rule acceptably to them, knowing that all governments— oligarchies as well as the others—have the longest life when they best serve the masses. You will be a wise leader of the people if you do not allow the multitude either to do or to suffer outrage, but see to it that the best among them shall have the honors, while the rest shall suffer no impairment of their rights; for these are the first and most important elements of good government.

—Isocrates, speech to Nicocles

Whoever shows his excellence in the case of his own household will be found righteous in his city as well.

—Sophocles, *Antigone*

A state's purpose is not merely to provide a living but to make a life that is good.

—Aristotle, *Politics*

I never yet feared those men who set a place apart in the middle of their cities where they gather to cheat one another and swear oaths which they break.

—Herodotus, *Histories*

To rule at all costs, not only justly but unjustly, is unlawful, and merely to have the upper hand is not necessarily to have a just title to it.

—Aristotle, *Politics*

Dangerous is a people's voice charged with wrath—it acts as a curse of publicly ratified doom.

—**Aeschylus,** *Agamemnon*

You should not consider it slavery to obey the government, but rather, freedom.

—**Aristides the Just**

The true champion of justice, if he intends to survive even for a short time, must necessarily confine himself to private life and leave politics alone.

—**Socrates, as quoted in Plato's** *Apology*

Each government has a peculiar character which originally formed and which continues to preserve it. The character of democracy creates democracy, and the character of oligarchy creates oligarchy.

—**Aristotle,** *Politics*

THE LAW

Do you imagine that a city can continue to exist and not be turned upside down if the legal judgments which are pronounced in it have no force but are nullified and destroyed by private persons?

—**Socrates, as quoted in Plato's** *Crito*

Which is most useful, to obey an excellent man or excellent laws?

—Aristotle, *Politics*

Laws are like spiders' webs. If some small and powerless thing falls in them, it is caught, but a bigger one can break through and get away.

—Solon, fragment

He that does no wrong is indeed a man worthy of honor; but worthy of twice as much honor as he, and more, is the man who, in addition, consents not to wrongdoers when they do wrong; for while the former counts as one man, the latter counts as many, in that he informs the magistrates of the wrongdoing of the rest.

—Plato, *Laws*

When you are just you use your character as law.

—Menander, fragment

Where the laws are not sovereign, there you find demagogues.

—Aristotle, *Politics*

As in a hospital where drugs and doctors abound are many diseases, in a city with many laws there is great injustice.

—Plato

He who injures no one hasn't any need of laws.
>—Plato

The people must fight on behalf of the law as though for the city's walls.
>—Heraclitus, as quoted by Diogenes Laërtius in *Lives of Eminent Philosophers*

Law is intelligence without appetite.
>—Aristotle, *Politics*

The freedom which we enjoy in our government extends also to our ordinary life. There, far from exercising a jealous surveillance over each other, we do not feel called upon to be angry with our neighbor for doing what he likes, or even to indulge in those injurious looks which cannot fail to be offensive, although they inflict no positive penalty. But all this ease in our private relations does not make us lawless as citizens. Against this fear is our chief safeguard, teaching us to obey the magistrates and the laws, particularly such as regard the protection of the injured, whether they are actually on the statute book, or belong to that code which, although unwritten, yet cannot be broken without acknowledged disgrace.
>—Pericles, "Funeral Oration," as quoted in Thucydides' *The History of the Peloponnesian War*

MONARCHY

In a monarchy, as its name indicates, one man alone is supreme over all; if it is subject to certain regulations, it is called a kingdom; if it is unlimited, a tyranny.

—Aristotle, *Rhetoric*

If anyone should hold that it is best for states to be ruled by kings, he will have to consider a question relating to the king's children. Are his offspring also to be kings? Considering what kind of persons some of these have turned out to be, we would have to say that hereditary succession is harmful. You may say the king, having sovereign power, will not in that case hand it over to his children. But it is hard to believe that: It is a difficult achievement, which expects too much virtue of human nature.

—Aristotle, *Politics*

Every king, every despot is the sworn foe of freedom and of law.

—Demosthenes, *Speeches*

The perversion of Kingship is Tyranny.

—Aristotle, *Nicomachean Ethics*

How can a monarchy be a suitable thing, which allows a man to do as he pleases with none to hold him to account? And even if you were to take the best man on earth, and put him into a monarchy, you put outside him the thoughts that usually guide him.

—Herodotus, *Histories*

SOCIETY

He who is unable to live in society or who has no need of it because he is sufficient for himself, must be either a beast or a god.

—**Aristotle,** *Politics*

There is no greater evil than anarchy.

—**Sophocles,** *Antigone*

A state is strongest when ruled by the counsels of old men and the fighting spirits of young men.

—**Pindar**

I hate that citizen, who, to help his fatherland,
seems slow, but swift to do great harm,
of profit to himself, but useless to the state.

—**Aristophanes,** *The Frogs*

There is nothing more foolish, nothing more given to outrage, than a useless mob.

—**Herodotus,** *Histories*

The primary classes of men are three: the philosopher or lover of wisdom, the lover of victory, and the lover of gain.

—**Plato,** *The Republic*

To leave the number of births unrestricted, as is done in most states, inevitably causes poverty among the citizens, and poverty produces faction and crime.

—**Aristotle,** *Politics*

Civil strife is as much a greater evil than a concerted war effort as war itself is worse than peace.

—**Herodotus,** *Histories*

TYRANNY AND REVOLUTION

A state is not a state if it belongs to one man.

—**Sophocles,** *Antigone*

Any excuse will serve a tyrant.

—**Aesop,** *Fables*

Inferiors revolt in order that they may be equal, and equals that they may be superior. Such is the state of mind which creates revolutions.

—**Aristotle,** *Politics*

Look at the orators in our republics; as long as they are poor, both state and people can only praise their uprightness; but once they are fattened on the public funds, they conceive a hatred for justice, plan intrigues against the people, and attack the democracy.

—**Aristophanes,** *Plutus*

Revolutions are not about trifles, but they spring from trifles.

—**Aristotle,** *Politics*

It is a disease that is somehow inherent in tyranny to have no faith in friends.

—**Aeschylus,** *Prometheus Bound*

The people always have some champion whom they set over them and nurse into greatness. . . . This and no other is the root from which a tyrant springs; when he first appears he is a protector.

—**Socrates, as quoted in Plato's** *The Republic*

[Regarding] major crimes, men commit them when their aims are extravagant, not just to provide themselves with necessities.

Whoever heard of a man making himself a dictator in order to keep warm? For this reason there is more honor in slaying a tyrant than a thief.

—**Aristotle,** *Politics*

Tragedies find a place among the rich and among kings and tyrants, but no poor man fills a tragic role except as a member of the chorus.

—**Epictetus,** *Discourses*

Often even a whole city suffers for a bad man who sins and contrives presumptuous deeds.

—**Hesiod,** *Works and Days*

GREAT MINDS
ON THE GREEKS

Of all that the Greeks did only a very small part has come down to us and we have no means of knowing if we have their best . . . But this little remnant preserved by the haphazard of chance shows the high-water mark reached in every region of thought and beauty the Greeks entered. No sculpture comparable to theirs; no buildings ever more beautiful; no writings superior. Prose, always late of development, they had time only to touch upon, but they left masterpieces. History has yet to find a greater exponent than Thucydides; outside the Bible there is no poetical prose that can touch Plato. In poetry they are all but supreme; no epic is to be mentioned with Homer; no odes to be set beside Pindar; of the four masters of the tragic stage three are Greek.

—Edith Hamilton, *The Greek Way*

If (according to Plutarch) a Philip did not disdain personally to direct the education of his son Alexander [the Great] and to give him the great Aristotle as a teacher, because he did not regard the ordinary teachers as adequate, if a Laudon personally directed the education of his son, why should not such great and exalted examples be emulated in our time?

—Ludwig Van Beethoven, from a letter to the Vienna magistracy

Just as Socrates felt that it was necessary to create a tension in the mind so that individuals could rise from the bondage of myths and half-truths to the unfettered realm of creative analysis and objective appraisal, we must see the need of having nonviolent gadflies to create the kind of tension in society that will help men to rise from the dark depths of prejudice and racism to the majestic heights of understanding and brotherhood.

—Martin Luther King, letter from a Birmingham jail

What Athens was in miniature America will be in magnitude. The one was the wonder of the ancient world; the other is becoming the admiration of the present.

Thomas Paine, *Rights of Man*

I like people who like Plato.

—Ralph Waldo Emerson, "Culture"

For thousands of years humans were oppressed—as some of us still are—by the notion that the universe is a marionette whose strings are pulled by a god or gods, unseen and inscrutable. Then, 2,500 years ago, there was a glorious awakening in Ionia: on Samos and the other nearby Greek colonies that grew up among the islands and inlets of the busy eastern Aegean Sea. Suddenly there were people who believed that everything was made of atoms; that human beings and other animals had sprung from simpler forms; that diseases were not caused by demons or the gods; that the Earth was only a planet going around the Sun. And that the stars were very far away. This revolution made Cosmos out of Chaos.

> —Carl Sagan, *Cosmos*

Other peoples have saints; the Greeks have sages.

> —Friedrich Nietzsche, *Philosophy in the Tragic Age of the Greeks*

While I was intent on improving my language, I met with an English grammar…at the end of which there were two little sketches of the arts of rhetoric and logic, the latter finishing with a specimen of a dispute in the Socratic method, and soon after I procured Xenophon's Memorable Things of Socrates, wherein there are many instances of the same method. I was charmed with it, adopted it, dropped my abrupt contradiction and positive argumentation, and put on the humble inquirer and doubter.

> —Benjamin Franklin, *The Autobiography of Benjamin Franklin*

Whatever, in fact, is modern in our life we owe to the Greeks. Whatever is an anachronism is due to mediaevalism.

—Oscar Wilde, "The Critic as Artist"

The mention of Greece fills the mind with the most exalted sentiments and arouses in our bosoms the best feelings of which our nature is capable.

—James Monroe, message to congress

Socrates . . . brought human wisdom back down from heaven, where she was wasting her time, and restored her to man. . . . It is impossible to go back further and lower. He did a great favor to human nature by showing how much it can do by itself.

—Michel de Montaigne, "Of Physiognomy"

The Greeks, with their truly healthy culture, have once and for all justified philosophy simply by having engaged in it, and engaged in it more fully than any other people.

—Friedrich Nietzsche, *Philosophy in the Tragic Age of the Greeks*

What is the foundation of that interest all men feel in Greek history, letters, art and poetry, in all its periods from the Heroic and Homeric age down to the domestic life of the Athenians and Spartans, four or five centuries later? What but this, that every man passes personally through a Grecian period.

—Ralph Waldo Emerson, "History"

As we turned and moved again through the temple, I wished that the illustrious men who had sat in it in the remote ages could visit it again and reveal themselves to our curious eyes—Plato, Aristotle, Demosthenes, Socrates, Phocion, Pythagoras, Euclid, Pindar, Xenophon, Herodotus, Praxiteles and Phidias, Zeuxis the painter. What a constellation of celebrated names! But more than all, I wished that old Diogenes, groping so patiently with his lantern, searching so zealously for one solitary honest man in all the world, might meander along and stumble on our party. I ought not to say it, may be, but still I suppose he would have put out his light.

—**Mark Twain,** *The Innocents Abroad*

Aristotle, and most of the other Greek philosophers, on the other hand, did not like the idea of a creation because it smacked too much of divine intervention. They believed, therefore, that the human race and the world around it had existed, and would exist, forever.

—**Stephen Hawking,** *A Brief History of Time*

The degree of moderation and humanity attained is exactly reflected in the humanization of the gods: The Greeks of the strongest epoch, who were not afraid of themselves but rejoiced in themselves, brought their gods close to all their own affects.

—**Friedrich Nietzsche,** *The Will to Power*

In nature, all is useful, all is beautiful. It is therefore beautiful, because it is alive, moving, reproductive; it is therefore useful, because it is symmetrical and fair. Beauty will not come at the call of a legislature, nor will it repeat in England or America its history in Greece. It will come, as always, unannounced, and spring up between the feet of brave and earnest men.

> —Ralph Waldo Emerson, "Art"

But it is fit that the past should be dark; though the darkness is not so much a quality of the past as of tradition. It is not a distance of time, but a distance of relation, which makes thus dusky its memorials. What is near to the heart of this generation is fair and bright still. Greece lies outspread fair and sunshiny in floods of light, for there is the sun and daylight in her literature and art. Homer does not allow us to forget that the sun shone—nor Phidias, nor the Parthenon.

> —Henry David Thoreau, *A Week on the Concord and Merrimack Rivers*

We see then how far the monuments of wit and learning are more durable than the monuments of power of the hands. For have not the verses of Homer continued twenty-five hundred years, or more, without the loss of a syllable or letter; during which time infinite palaces, temples, castles, cities, have been decayed and demolished?

> —Francis Bacon, *The Advancement of Learning*

TIME LINE OF ANCIENT GREECE

(all dates B.C.E)

circa 1600 — Island of Thera explodes, causing a tidal wave that destroys the civilization of Crete

circa 1300 — Theseus establishes the city of Athens

circa 1250 — Troy falls to the Greek army after a ten-year siege

circa 1200 — Dorians set up states in the southern Peloponnesus, Crete, and Rhodes

circa 800 — Lycurgus institutes reforms in Sparta. Homer composes *The Iliad* and *The Odyssey*

776 — First Olympic Games

circa 733 — Syracuse is founded by Corinth

594 — Solon gives Athens a constitutional democracy and wipes out all citizen debts which, up to that point, had led to indentured slavery

560–527 — Tyranny of Pisistratus and his sons in Athens. Eventually this period is ended by the coming of Cleisthenes

490 — Battle of Marathon. Athens defeats the Persian army

480 — King Xerxes of Persia invades Greece. Persian forces overcome the heroic resistance of

a vastly outnumbered Spartan force at the Battle of Thermopylae. Athens is destroyed. At the Battle of Salamis the Persian navy is destroyed by the Greeks and Xerxes decides to retreat and leave his lieutenant, Mardonius, to finish the campaign

479 Battle of Plataea. Allied Greek forces defeat the Persians under Mardonius, and the Persian invasion is terminated in utter defeat for the Medes

477 Athens assumes leadership of the Delian League, an alliance of the city-states and islands of Greece against the Persians

454 Treasury of the Delian League is transferred to Athens

443 Thucydides ostracized, leaving Pericles in total control of Athens. The Athenians embezzle the treasury

of the Delian League to build the Parthenon and other monuments

431 Peloponnesian War begins. Athens and Sparta struggle for hegemony

429 Pericles dies of the plague in Athens

421 Peace of Nicias begins, temporarily ending the Peloponnesian War

415 Peace of Nicias ends, and Athens invades Sicily

413 Nicias and the Athenian army surrender in Sicily

405 Dionysius I becomes tyrant of Syracuse

404 Peloponnesian War ends when Athens surrenders to Sparta. Tyranny of the Thirty begins in Athens

401–399	Greek mercenaries, including Xenophon, fight their way through the Persian Empire to the Black Sea (March of the Ten Thousand)
399	Socrates is sentenced to death in Athens
382	Sparta seizes Thebes by surprise attack
379	Pelopidas liberates Thebes
371	Spartan power is crushed by Thebes at the Battle of Leuctra
362	Battle of Mantinea; Epaminondas dies
338	Battle of Chaeronea. King Philip II of Macedonia defeats the allied armies of the Greeks and becomes ruler of Greece
336	Alexander the Great becomes king of Macedonia after Philip's assassination.
335	Alexander destroys Thebes
333	Battle of Issus. Alexander defeats the Persian army and takes control of half of the Persian Empire
331	Battle of Gaugamela. Alexander defeats King Darius and takes control of the whole Persian Empire. Greek language and civilization spread from Egypt to India
326	Battle of the Hydaspes. Alexander's invasion of India ends
323	Alexander enters Babylon and dies
318	The Athenians sentence Phocion to death
301	Alexander's successors fight at the Battle of Ipsus

BIOGRAPHIES OF PROMINENT GREEKS

Aeschylus (525–456 B.C.E.)
Athenian tragedian. He fought at the Battle of Marathon and at Salamis, Artemisium, and Plataea against the Persians. Aeschylus wrote over eighty plays, of which only seven survive. Among his best-known plays are *Seven Against Thebes, The Persians,* and *Prometheus Bound.* He is often credited with inventing the tragedy.

Aesop (c. 620–560 B.C.E.)
Storyteller. He was born a Thracian slave and later in his life lived on the island of Samos. His fables were known throughout Greece. His influence on Greek education and culture is significant. In his fables Aesop uses didactic examples and fiction involving animals, nature, and human society.

Agesilaus II (445–359 B.C.E.)
King of Sparta. Considered one of Sparta's greatest military leaders. In 396 B.C.E. Agesilaus II led Spartan forces to a crushing victory over the Persian governor of Asia Minor, Tissaphernes.

Agis
King of Sparta. Son of Agesilaus II. He became king about 427 B.C.E.

Alexander III (the Great) (356–323 B.C.E.)

King of Macedonia. Son of Philip II and pupil of Aristotle. In revenge for the Persian Wars against Greece, Alexander invaded and destroyed the Persian Empire with an army of forty thousand Greek soldiers. His kingdom extended from Greece to India. Alexander was responsible for the spread of the Greek language and customs throughout the then-known world. He left no heirs and his kingdom was eventually taken over by the Romans within three hundred years of his death.

Anaxagoras (c. 500–428 B.C.E.)

Philosopher. Teacher of Pericles and Euripides. He taught that the intellect, *nous,* is the central guiding force in the universe. He also believed that the intellect is the animating force in both animals and vegetables.

Anaximander (c. 610–c. 545 B.C.E.)

Philosopher. He taught that the universe is infinite, consisting of countless worlds. He was the first to speculate about the sizes of the sun and moon as well as their distances from Earth.

Anaximenes of Miletus (c. sixth century B.C.E.)

Philosopher. Pupil of Anaximander. He taught that the world is derived from condensed air and that the cosmos comes into and out of existence in a cyclical manner.

Archimedes (c. 287–211 B.C.E.)

Inventor and mathematician. Credited with inventing hydrostatic principles, hydraulic devices, and defense weapons. Cicero reports that

Archimedes had made two spheres depicting the planets and stars and referred to them as a "planetarium" and a "star globe."

Aristides (c. fifth century B.C.E.)

Athenian statesman. Also known as Aristedes the Just. He was a general at the battles of Marathon, Salamis, and Plataea against the Persians. He was ostracized and banished from Athens in 490 B.C.E. after helping the Athenians win the Battle of Marathon. Together with Cimon he set up the Delian League. He died in complete penury c. 460 B.C.E.

Aristophanes (c. 445–c. 385 B.C.E.)

Comic poet. His plays are of a satirical nature, caricaturing real-life characters. His surviving plays include *Lysistrata, The Clouds, The Knights, The Acharnians, The Wasps, The Birds, The Thesmophoriazusae, The Frogs, Assemblywomen,* and *Wealth.*

Aristotle (384–322 B.C.E.)

Philosopher. One of the greatest philosophers and scientists of all time. He was born in Stagyra, in northern Greece, and at the age of seventeen joined Plato's Academy in Athens. Plato's sobriquet for his student was "the mind of the Academy." After Plato's death Aristotle left Athens. He was hired by Philip II to tutor his son Alexander (the Great). After Philip's death, Aristotle moved back to Athens, where he founded the Lyceum, a philosophic academy complete with a gymnasium and a library. He wrote on nearly every topic and every science. Among his surviving works are *Physics, Metaphysics, Eudemian Ethics, Nicomachean Ethics, Politics, Magna Moralia, Rhetoric,* and *Poetics.*

Arrian (c. 86–160 C.E.)

Historian. A friend and pupil of Epictetus. He wrote an account of the expedition of Alexander the Great against the Persian Empire, entitled *Anabasis of Alexander.*

Brasidas (c. fourth century B.C.E.)

General. He was born in Sparta and led his city-state against Athens in the Peloponnesian War. Thucydides ranks him above all Spartan commanders.

Callicrates (c. fifth century B.C.E.)

Architect. Together with Ictinus he designed the Parthenon. He also designed the sanctuary of Nike and the central wall of the Acropolis.

Cimon (c. 510–450 B.C.E.)

Athenian statesman and general. He was the son of Miltiades. Together with Aristides he founded the Delian League, an organization created to protect Greek city-states from Persian aggression. In 467 B.C.E. he led the Athenian fleet to the destruction of the entire Persian fleet in what is known as the Eurymedon campaign.

Cleisthenes (c. fifth century B.C.E.)

Athenian statesman. One of Athens's most important constitutional reformers. He introduced a representative system which included ten tribes, representing the entire population of Athens, and a lawmaking council of five hundred, the Boule. Cleisthenes also introduced ostracism, by which excessively powerful citizens, possibly tyrants, could be exiled after a referendum.

Democritus (c. 460–356 B.C.E.)

Philosopher and scientist. His research included physics, mathematics, and music. Together with Leucippus, Democritus is credited with the development of the atomic theory. The two scientists, also called "atomists," believed that the cosmos is made up of minute, indivisible elements called "atoms." Democritus taught that by joining together, atoms are responsible for the creation of solid, liquid, and gaseous objects. Democritus also believed in the existence of other worlds, similar to Earth.

Demosthenes (384–322 B.C.E.)

Athenian orator. His speeches are a cynosure for modern oratory. His influence on Athenian politics and foreign policy was catalytic in developments in Greece in the fourth century B.C.E.. Demosthenes delivered many orations against King Philip II of Macedonia when the latter attempted to unite all the Greek city-states under Macedonian rule. He was renowned for clarity of thought and precise use of language.

Diogenes of Sinope (c. 400–c. 323 B.C.E.)

Philosopher. Also known as "the Cynic." He practiced extreme self-denial and asceticism. Diogenes taught that through self-abnegation and strict avoidance of self-indulgence a person could become virtuous and, ultimately, happy. There are many anecdotes about Diogenes' life. It is said that he once went about Athens carrying a lantern in broad daylight searching for an honest man.

Diogenes Laërtius (early third century C.E.)

Biographer. His *Lives of Eminent Philosophers* rescued for posterity the teachings of most Greek philosophers and scientists.

Draco (c. seventh century B.C.E.)

Athenian lawmaker. His penal code was extremely harsh. He instituted the death penalty for many offenses. The adjective "draconian," very severe, was coined after his laws.

Empedocles (c. 493–433 B.C.E.)

Philosopher. He taught that the universe is spherical in shape and composed of four basic elements: earth, water, fire, and air. He also researched and wrote about various physical phenomena.

Epaminondas (c. 418–362 B.C.E.)

General from Thebes. He led Theban forces to an unprecedented victory over the Spartans at Leuctra in 371 B.C.E.

Epictetus (c. 55–c. 135 C.E.)

Stoic philosopher. Formerly a slave. He attended philosophical lectures in Rome. Arrian, Epictetus' pupil, wrote eight books entitled *Discourses,* and a philosophical treatise, *Enchiridion,* which popularized his mentor's teachings. Epictetus taught that man ought to use his intellect and will to make moral decisions and that corrupt people were injuring themselves more than their victims and should be treated with clemency rather than with severity.

Epicurus (341–270 B.C.E.)

Philosopher. He wrote more than three hundred books on topics ranging from moral philosophy to physics and epistemology. He taught that the human soul does not survive the body's death and that the gods, even though they exist, do not govern fate or destiny.

Eratosthenes (c. 276–c.194 B.C.E.)

Geographer and mathematician. In his book, *Geographica,* he gives an accurate measurement of the earth's circumference and also describes the sizes of the moon and the sun and their distances from earth.

Euclid (late fourth century B.C.E.)

Mathematician. He wrote thirteen volumes on plane geometry and mathematics. He also indited the treatises on musical theory entitled *Introduction to Harmony* and *Section of the Scale.*

Euripides (c. 484–406 B.C.E.)

Tragedian. He won numerous first prizes in various theatrical contests and, together with Aeschylus and Sophocles, is considered one of the greatest dramatists of all time. He wrote eighty plays, of which only nineteen survive. Among those are *Iphigenia in Tauris, Hippolytus, The Trojan Women, Rhesus,* and *Alcestis.*

Hecataeus (late sixth century B.C.E.)

Geographer. He wrote a treatise on geography entitled *Guide to the Earth* and two books entitled *Europe* and *Asia.*

Heraclitus (c. 540–c. 480 B.C.E.)

Philosopher. Born in Ephesus. Also known as "the Obscure." He wrote philosophical aphorisms. Heraclitus taught that the cosmos is in a state of perpetual change. He believed that fire was the most dominant element and that it gave life to all living things.

Herodotus (484–c. 425 B.C.E.)

Historian. He traveled extensively around the then-known world. His work, *Histories,* is the culmination of his travels and knowledge of the conflicts between the Greeks and Persians known as the Persian Wars. Through Herodotus we have an intimate knowledge of non-European cultures and customs during the fifth century B.C.E.

Hesiod (early seventh century B.C.E.)

Poet. A contemporary of Homer. His works, *Theogony* and *Works and Days,* greatly influenced later Greek generations. His didactic approach is replete with moral and practical lessons about the life a Greek farmer ought to live.

Hippocrates (c. fifth century B.C.E.)

Physician. Considered the father of medicine. Many ancient medical texts and treatises bear his name but it is believed that most of them were written by physicians who wanted to add authority to their work. He was a proponent of healthful eating and hygiene for the achievement of a healthy body. His Hippocratic Oath is still admin- istered to graduating doctors throughout the United States and Europe.

Homer (c. eighth century B.C.E.)

Poet. One of the greatest epic poets of all time. His *Iliad* and *Odyssey* are still read today in high schools and universities around the world. In 540 B.C.E. Peisistratus, ruler of Athens, is said to have ordered the transcription of the two poems which, up to that time, were passed orally from one generation of bards to the other. In

The Iliad, the Greek army has laid siege to Troy because Paris, one of the king Priam of Troy's sons, has abducted Helen, the wife of Menelaus, the powerful ruler of Sparta. In *The Odyssey,* Homer describes king of Ithaca Odysseus' voyage home after the sacking and destruction of Troy. Both works are examples of some of the finest poetry ever composed. Also attributed to Homer are *Homeric Hymns, Epic Cycle,* and *Battle of Frogs and Mice.*

Ictinus (c. fifth century B.C.E.)

Architect. Together with Callicrates he designed the Parthenon in 447 B.C.E.

Isocrates (436–338 B.C.E.)

Athenian speechwriter. Founder of an influential academy of rhetoric in Athens around the time of Plato, Isocrates was also a contemporary and, possibly, an acquaintance of Socrates. Like Demosthenes, Isocrates exerted heavy influence upon Athenian politics and foreign policy. Twenty-one of his speeches survive.

Leonidas I (c. fifth century B.C.E.)

King of Sparta. In 480 B.C.E. he faced the Persian army at Thermopylae with an army of three hundred Spartan and seven hundred Thespian soldiers. For two days his army withstood the relentless attack of the Persians. When Ephialtes betrayed the Greeks by showing the Persians a secret passage through which they could surround Leonidas and his army, both Spartans and Thespians decided to stay and fight to the very end. King Leonidas' heroic death has been an example of courage and ultimate self-sacrifice.

Lycurgus (c. ninth century B.C.E.)
Spartan lawmaker. Credited with having created Sparta's constitution, known as the Great Rhetra.

Menander (c. 343–292 B.C.E.)
Playwright. He wrote over one hundred comedies, of which mostly fragments survive.

Miltiades (c. 550–489 B.C.E.)
Athenian statesman. The victorious general against the Persians at the Battle of Marathon. He died a short time after his victory from an injury he sustained in a campaign against the island of Paros.

Pericles (c. 495–429 B.C.E.)
Athenian statesman. Responsible for rebuilding Athens after the Persian Wars. The Parthenon, the Propylaia, and the Erectheum on the Acropolis were built during Pericles' term. He conceptualized the Delian League, an organization of Greek city-states created to protect Greece from future Persian attacks.

Philip II (382–336 B.C.E.)
King of Macedonia. Father of Alexander the Great. Responsible for uniting Greece under his rule. His planned invasion of Persia was prevented by his assassination in 336 B.C.E.

Pindar (c. 518–c. 438 B.C.E.)
Poet. His odes are touchstones of Greek lyric poetry and most were composed to celebrate victors at the Olympic, Nemean, Pythian, and

Isthmian games. His florid prose style and adroit use of metaphor and allegory won him a place at the top of the Greek lyric-poet list.

Plato (c. 427–347 B.C.E.)

Philosopher. Mentor of Aristotle and friend of Socrates. Through his works Plato was responsible for preserving Socrates' memory and teachings. Plato's dialogues are composed as conversations between friends and colleagues in an attempt by the author to "lighten up" the heavy philosophical questions examined. His theory of forms, the theory that there exists a complete cosmos of ideas, or forms, on which our material universe is based, influenced later generations of philosophers. Plato wrote on various ethical, political, and philosophical topics. Among his extant works are the so-called "Socratic" dialogues *Euthyphro, Apology, Crito,* and *Phaedo,* which narrate Socrates' trial and execution, *The Republic, Laws,* and *Symposium,* as well as letters to colleagues.

Plutarch (c. 46 C.E.–c. 121C.E.)

Biographer. His *Lives* give a unique account of the lives and accomplishments of noted Greek and Roman statesmen and provide a moral compass for educating the young. He also wrote on various ethical and pedagogic matters in his essays entitled *Moralia.*

Pyrrhus (319–272 B.C.E.)

King of Epirus. Cousin of Alexander the Great. He led several campaigns against Macedonia and Rome. His victory at Heraclea in 281 B.C.E. against the Roman consul Laevinus came at such devastating cost to his army as to coin the term "Pyrrhic victory."

Pythagoras (c. sixth century B.C.E.)

Philosopher and mathematician. He founded an academy at Croton, in southern Italy. There, he took both men and women as pupils and some of his best students were women. Pythagoras' followers were secretive about his teachings and practiced a strict form of vegetarianism. Pythagoras interpreted the universe through numbers. He discovered the musical scale. His mathematics influenced philosophers such as Plato, and his Pythagorean Theorem is today taught throughout the world.

Sappho (c. late seventh century B.C.E.)

Poetess. From the island of Lesbos. Her verse is powerful and intimate. The prominent theme in her erotic poems is the love of a woman for another woman. She also composed hymns to the goddess Aphrodite. She is thought to have been a mentor to a group of female friends.

Socrates (469–399 B.C.E.)

Philosopher from Athens. Veteran of the battles at Delium and Amphipolis. Socrates himself did not write down his teachings. They were transcribed later on by his pupil Plato and by Xenophon. His dialectic method was based on a question-and-answer process known as *élenchos,* examination. Socrates taught that anyone interested in learning would have to first discard everything he believed he knew—but in reality did not—before real knowledge could be attained. Socrates felt it was his moral duty as a philosopher and citizen to wake Athenians to this reality. In 399 B.C.E. he was found guilty of introducing "false gods" in his teachings and after a trial was executed by having to drink hemlock.

Solon (c. 639–c. 559 B.C.E.)

Athenian statesman. A nobleman by birth, he abolished indentured slavery and revised most of Draco's strict laws. Solon not only freed Athenian citizens who had made themselves slaves by failing to repay their debts but bought back Athenians who had been sold as slaves abroad. He divided Athens into four classes based on their property and wealth. Everyone had the right to attend the state council, the so-called Council of the Four Hundred. Solon allowed all Athenians to participate in trials as jurors. He was regarded as the father of Athenian democracy and he paved the road for Cleisthenes. He was also one of the Seven Sages of Ancient Greece.

Sophocles (c. 496–406 B.C.E.)

Athenian tragedian. Together with Aeschylus and Euripides is considered to be one of the greatest tragic poets of antiquity. He wrote 123 plays, of which only seven survive. Among his extant plays are *Antigone, Philoctetes, Oedipus Rex, Ajax,* and *Oedipus at Colonus.* Aristotle referred to *Oedipus Rex* as the perfect tragedy.

Strabo (c. 64 B.C.E.–24 B.C.E.)

Geographer. The writer of many books on geography and topography, Strabo traveled widely around Africa and Europe. His main work, *Geography,* composed of seventeen books, still survives.

Thales of Miletus (c. 625–547 B.C.E.)

Philosopher. Ancient philosophers and scientists credited Thales with extraordinary scientific feats such as the measurement of the height of the pyramids and the calculation of solstices. He was believed to be an innovator in many sciences and was one of the Seven Sages of Ancient Greece.

Themistocles (c. 524–459 B.C.E.)

Statesman. Victor of the Battle of Salamis, Themistocles was responsible for the destruction of the Persian navy and, afterward, for the fortification of Athens. He was ostracized and exiled to Argos. He ended up in Persia, where in 459 B.C.E. is believed to have committed suicide after being asked by Persian King Artaxerxes to betray Greece.

Theognis (c. sixth century B.C.E.)

Poet from Megara. About fourteen hundred verses of his exist today in fragments. Theognis includes moral and aristocratic elements in his poetry.

Thucydides (c. 455–c. 400 B.C.E.)

Historian. He documented the Peloponnesian War. Even though he was born an aristocrat, Thucydides was an ardent admirer of democracy and Pericles. Pericles' "Funeral Oration," as written by Thucydides, is an oratorical masterpiece that serves to evoke a sense of patriotism and civic duty as well as describe the greatness of Athens after the victories in the Persian Wars. His methodology, accurately describing historical events and using authentic sources, has served as a benchmark for later generations of historians.

Xenophon (c. 428–354 B.C.E.)

Historian. An associate of Socrates, Xenophon fought in Cyrus' army against Cyrus' older brother, Artaxerxes, in the Battle of Cunaxa in

401 B.C.E. Cyrus was defeated and killed. Xenophon's adventures in reaching Greece from the midst of Asia after the defeat are documented in his *March of the Ten Thousand*. He also wrote a history of Greece entitled *Hellenica,* the memoirs of Socrates, *Memorabilia,* as well as a dialogue on estate management, entitled *Oeconomicus.*

Zeno of Elea (c. 490–454 B.C.E.)

Philosopher. Regarded as the founder of the dialectical argument. He is famous for propounding paradoxes on plurality, motion, predication, and place.

Zeno of Citium (335–263 B.C.E.)

Philosopher. Founder of Stoicism, Zeno opened a school in Athens where he taught logic, ethics, and metaphysics. Zeno maintained that virtue is the ultimate good and that in order to achieve happiness one would first have to be virtuous.

SUGGESTED READING

Aeschylus, with an English translation by Herbert Weir Smyth, Ph. D., in 2 volumes, Vol. 1, *Prometheus Bound*. Cambridge, Mass.: Harvard University Press, 1926.

Aristotle. *Athenian Constitution. Virtues and Vices.* Aristotle in 23 volumes, Vol. 20, translated by H. Rackham. Cambridge, Mass.: Harvard University Press; London: William Heinemann Ltd., 1952.

Aristotle. *Metaphysics.* Aristotle in 23 volumes, Vols.17, 18, translated by Hugh Tredennick. Cambridge, Mass.: Harvard University Press; London: William Heinemann Ltd., 1933, 1989.

Aristotle. *Nicomachean Ethics.* Aristotle in 23 volumes, Vol. 19, translated by H. Rackham. Cambridge, Mass.: Harvard University Press; London: William Heinemann Ltd., 1934.

Aristotle. *Poetics.* Aristotle in 23 volumes, Vol. 23, translated by W. H. Fyfe. Cambridge, Mass.: Harvard University Press; London: William Heinemann Ltd., 1932.

Aristotle. *Politics.* Aristotle in 23 volumes, Vol. 21, translated by H. Rackham. Cambridge, Mass.: Harvard University Press; London: William Heinemann Ltd., 1944.

Euripides. *The Complete Greek Drama,* edited by Whitney J. Oates and Eugene O'Neill, Jr., in 2 volumes, Vol. 2, *Electra,* translated by E. P. Coleridge. New York: Random House, 1938.

Euripides. *The Complete Greek Drama,* edited by Whitney J. Oates and Eugene O'Neill, Jr., in 2 volumes, Vol. 1, *Iphigenia in Tauris,* translated by Robert Potter. New York: Random House, 1938.

Hamilton, Edith. *The Greek Way.* New York: W. W. Norton and Company, 1993.

Herodotus. *Histories,* with an English translation by A. D. Godley. Cambridge, Mass.: Harvard University Press, 1920.

Hesiod. *The Homeric Hymns* and *Homerica,* with an English translation by Hugh G. Evelyn-White. *Works and Days.* Cambridge, Mass.: Harvard University Press; London: William Heinemann Ltd., 1914.

Homer. *The Iliad,* with an English translation by A. T. Murray, Ph.D., in 2 volumes. Cambridge, Mass.: Harvard University Press; London: William Heinemann, Ltd., 1924.

Homer. *The Odyssey,* with an English translation by A. T. Murray, Ph.D., in 2 volumes. Cambridge, Mass.: Harvard University Press; London: William Heinemann, Ltd., 1919.

Isocrates, with an English translation in 3 volumes, by George Norlin, Ph.D., LL.D. Cambridge, Mass.: Harvard University Press; London: William Heinemann Ltd., 1980.

Kirk, G. S. and Raven, J. E. *The Presocratic Philosophers.* London: Cambridge University Press, 1962.

Pausanias. *Description of Greece,* with an English translation by W.H.S. Jones, Litt.D., and H. A. Ormerod, M.A., in 4 volumes. Cambridge, Mass.: Harvard University Press; London: William Heinemann Ltd., 1918.

Plato. *Euthyphro, Apology, Crito, Phaedo,* in 12 volumes, Vol. 1 translated by Harold North Fowler; Introduction by W.R.M. Lamb. Cambridge, Mass., Harvard University Press; London: William Heinemann Ltd., 1966.

Plato. *Laws,* in 12 volumes, Vols. 10, 11 translated by R. G. Bury. Cambridge, Mass.: Harvard University Press; London: William Heinemann Ltd., 1967 & 1968.

Plato. *Republic,* in 12 volumes, Vols. 5, 6 translated by Paul Shorey. Cambridge, Mass.: Harvard University Press; London: William Heinemann Ltd., 1969.

Plutarch. *Lives,* with an English translation by Bernadotte Perrin. Cambridge, Mass.: Harvard University Press. London: William Heinemann Ltd., 1914.

Sagan, Carl. *Cosmos.* New York: Random House, 1980.

Sophocles. *The Antigone of Sophocles,* edited with an introduction and notes by Sir Richard Jebb. Cambridge: Cambridge University Press, 1891.

Sophocles. *The Electra of Sophocles,* edited with introduction and notes by Sir Richard Jebb. Cambridge: Cambridge University Press, 1894.

Sophocles. *The Oedipus Tyrannus of Sophocles,* edited with an introduction and notes by Sir Richard Jebb. Cambridge: Cambridge University Press, 1887.

Strabo. *The Geography of Strabo,* edited by H. L. Jones. Cambridge, Mass.: Harvard University Press; London: William Heinemann, Ltd., 1924.

Thucydides. *The Peloponnesian War.* Richard Crawley. London: J. M. Dent; New York, E. P. Dutton, 1910.

Xenophon. *Xenophon in Seven Volumes,* Vol. 3, Carleton L. Brownson. Cambridge, Mass.: Harvard University Press; London: William Heinemann, Ltd., 1980.

ACKNOWLEDGMENTS

I would like to thank everyone who helped me through this extraordinary process known as publishing one's work. It was hard work, involving energy expenditure and dedication by many people.

My most sincere and warm acknowledgment goes to my loving wife, Ifigenia, who supported and helped me in more ways than I can ever explain. Without her vision this book wouldn't have been possible.

I would be ungrateful if I didn't thank my parents, Nicholas and Maria, who gave me an education and the tools to succeed in life.

Finally, we should all be grateful to the ancient historians, librarians, and writers who preserved the literary treasures of ancient Greece and passed on to us an incredible trove of thought and knowledge. They passed on to our generation a mirror wherein we can view our very souls.